PRAISE FOR TEVA HARRISON AND *IN-*

"Beautiful, heartbreaking, honest, and true, *In-Between L[...]* means to live with terminal cancer, but what it means to live with integrity in the face of our mortality. I couldn't put it down."

—Alison Pick, author of *Between Gods* and *Far to Go*

"With great wisdom, Teva Harrison understands that her cancer doesn't make her special. But this book certainly does. Through her art and her words, we are reminded of the power of creativity, and that hope for the future is an essentially creative act."

—Andrew Westoll, author of *The Chimps of Fauna Sanctuary*

"Teva Harrison's diagnosis with incurable cancer removes the expectation of an abundance of more—more dreams fulfilled, more time—but focuses her attention on the near and immediate. In this honest and raw memoir, Harrison examines and discovers, grieves and celebrates, and takes us with her as she crafts a ragged and resonant beauty from her experience in these *In-Between Days*."   —Miranda Hill, author of *Sleeping Funny*

"How does a person live with meaning—and joy—in the face of a terminal cancer diagnosis? Teva Harrison answers this question with pitch-perfect honesty and clarity, even when delving into her own complex contradictions. From Harrison's rigorous honesty comes wisdom. *In-Between Days* is a beautiful offering. This book fills my heart. The world is lucky to have Teva Harrison. She truly knows how to live, and to love."

—Angie Abdou, author of *Between*

"Teva's art and reflections powerfully capture the struggles of being young and facing the certain, yet uncertain, end of your life. May we all be this honest with ourselves as we deal with life's challenges. Inspiring, insightful, contemplative. Thank you, Teva."

—Geoff Eaton, Executive Director, Young Adult Cancer Canada

"There's no real preparation for how hard Teva Harrison's stunning graphic novel will hit you. It doesn't humanize the disease—that would be banal—and it doesn't aggrandize the journey—that would be self-help bunk. Rather, it portrays the process as something achingly human, a daily tumult of stuff that roughly amounts to survival. Teva Harrison has stared into the abyss. And what has stared back but love?"

—Richard Poplak, author of *Ja No Man*

"Teva Harrison is a metastatic voice that I believe is breaking through. By using humour and creativity to draw people in to a challenging topic, Teva is expanding the breast cancer conversation and shedding light on the complexities and nuances of the disease. I believe *In-Between Days* will help improve public understanding as well as empower and support others dealing with metastatic breast cancer. Beautifully done."

—MJ DeCoteau, Founder and Executive Director of ReThink Breast Cancer

In-Between Days

Days

a memoir about living with cancer

Teva Harrison

ANANSI

Published in Canada in 2016 by House of Anansi Press Inc.
www.houseofanansi.com

House of Anansi Press is committed to protecting our natural environment. As part of our efforts, the interior of this book is printed on paper that contains 100% post-consumer recycled fibres, is acid-free, and is processed chlorine-free.

20 19 18 17 16   1 2 3 4 5

Library and Archives Canada Cataloguing in Publication

Harrison, Teva, 1976–, author
In-between days : a memoir about living with cancer / Teva Harrison.

Issued in print and electronic formats.
ISBN 978-1-4870-0108-7 (paperback).—ISBN 978-1-4870-0109-4 (pdf)

1. Harrison, Teva, 1976– —Health—Comic books, strips, etc. 2. Breast—Cancer—Patients—Biography—Comic books, strips, etc. 3. Graphic novels. I. Title.

RC280.B8H37 2016   362.19699'4490092   C2015-908321-4
C2015-908322-2

Cover and text design: Alysia Shewchuk
Cover illustration: Teva Harrison

Canada Council for the Arts   Conseil des Arts du Canada
ONTARIO ARTS COUNCIL
CONSEIL DES ARTS DE L'ONTARIO
an Ontario government agency
un organisme du gouvernement de l'Ontario

We acknowledge for their financial support of our publishing program the Canada Council for the Arts, the Ontario Arts Council, and the Government of Canada through the Canada Book Fund.

Printed and bound in Canada

For David, who lifts me up

For my family and my ancestors

For the friends who step in
and make my life possible

For all people living with metastatic cancer,
as well as we can

CONTENTS

Preface

Drawing Forward

At the age of thirty-seven, I was diagnosed with advanced metastatic breast cancer. My disease is currently incurable, but the wonderful people in my medical team are doing everything they can to turn it into a chronic illness.

In order to make sense of what is happening to my body, I started seeing a psychiatrist within the psychosocial oncology team at my hospital. Talking about cancer turned into talking about my past, about my childhood and the coping mechanisms I'd developed, not all of which I'd call healthy. I'd leave his office churning with complicated emotions.

Back home, all worked up and raw, I started to draw my worst memories, my lived nightmares. An exorcism of sorts. I found myself drawing dark, primitive comics, and then I'd feel a bit of peace. Once the story was outside of my head, I could let go a little.

When I showed these illustrations to my doctor, he was so pleased. He encouraged me to keep drawing and see where it took me.

The brain is a tangle of memory, feeling, hope, and dream. Pull on a thread and it all unravels. In order to make sense of my cancer, I found myself working through all the buried, unresolved hurt and memory from my life before cancer.

It took months of drawing about my childhood before I even started to draw about my experience living with the disease.

I've been an artist my whole life, but this is the first time I have felt the need for narrative. Figuring out how to tell my story with comic strips has been interesting and empowering. When I was first diagnosed, I didn't want to talk to anybody. I've since learned that it's the unspoken that is most frightening. Shining a light on my experiences takes some of the power away from the bogeyman that is my cancer. I'm taking my power back.

I hope that by talking about some of the hard stuff, I am helping other people who are living with cancer or other serious illnesses (and their caregivers and supporters) to start conversations with peers and professionals, with their friends and family, and with their doctors.

Teva Harrison
Toronto, Ontario
December 2015

IN-BETWEEN DAYS

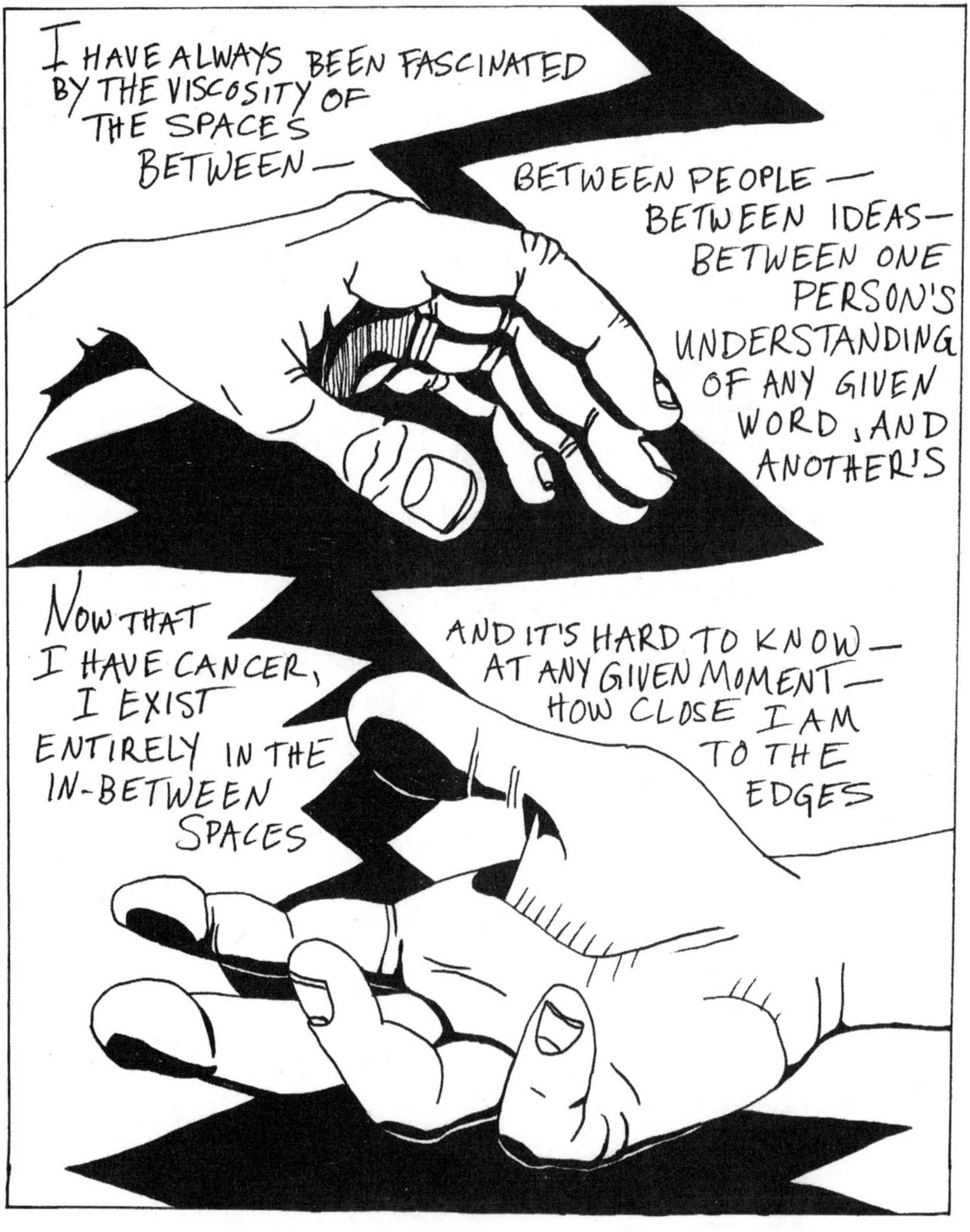
I HAVE ALWAYS BEEN FASCINATED BY THE VISCOSITY OF THE SPACES BETWEEN—
BETWEEN PEOPLE— BETWEEN IDEAS— BETWEEN ONE PERSON'S UNDERSTANDING OF ANY GIVEN WORD, AND ANOTHER'S
NOW THAT I HAVE CANCER, I EXIST ENTIRELY IN THE IN-BETWEEN SPACES
AND IT'S HARD TO KNOW— AT ANY GIVEN MOMENT— HOW CLOSE I AM TO THE EDGES

15 October 2016

For Liz —
Wishing you all the
joy & wonder in this
moment (& the next!)
x TEVA

In-Between Days

I occupy the liminal spaces, slipping between unnoticed.

The hours of cancer are strange. MRIs at 3:00 a.m., pain at 2:00 a.m., capable one day, incapable the next.

It's like living in the shadows.

And so I take the spaces nobody claims and I occupy them in the best way I know how: living life with a sense of wonder and delight.

Because I don't know how long I get to bask in the glory of this world and the people I love.

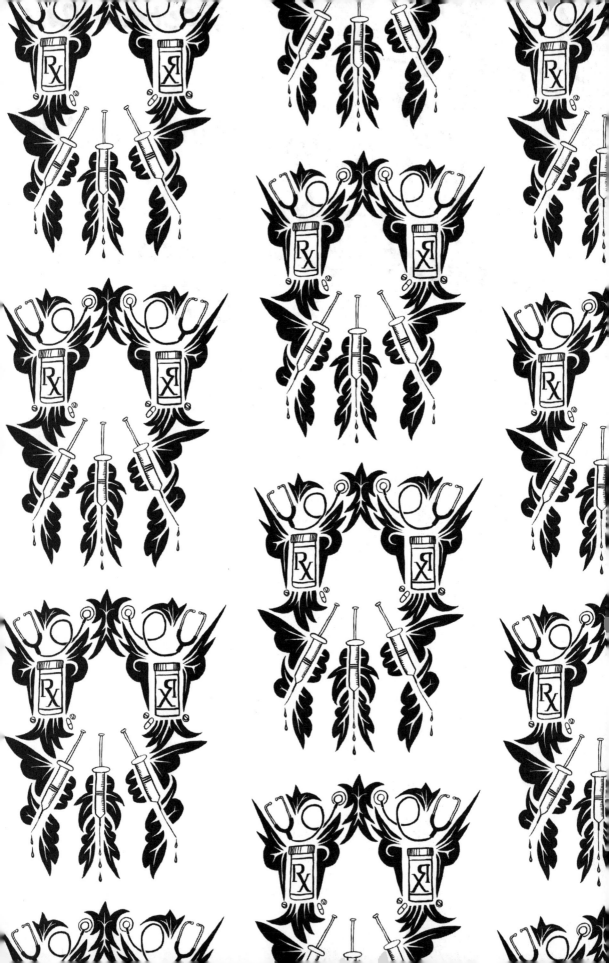

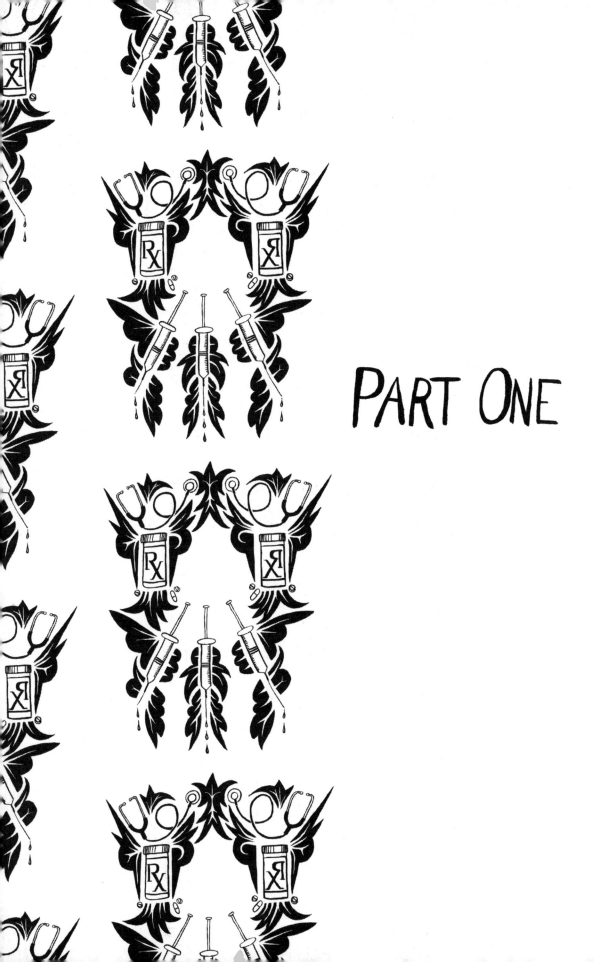

PART ONE

Diagnosis

LEARNING THAT I AM GOING TO DIE

What's Wrong With Me?

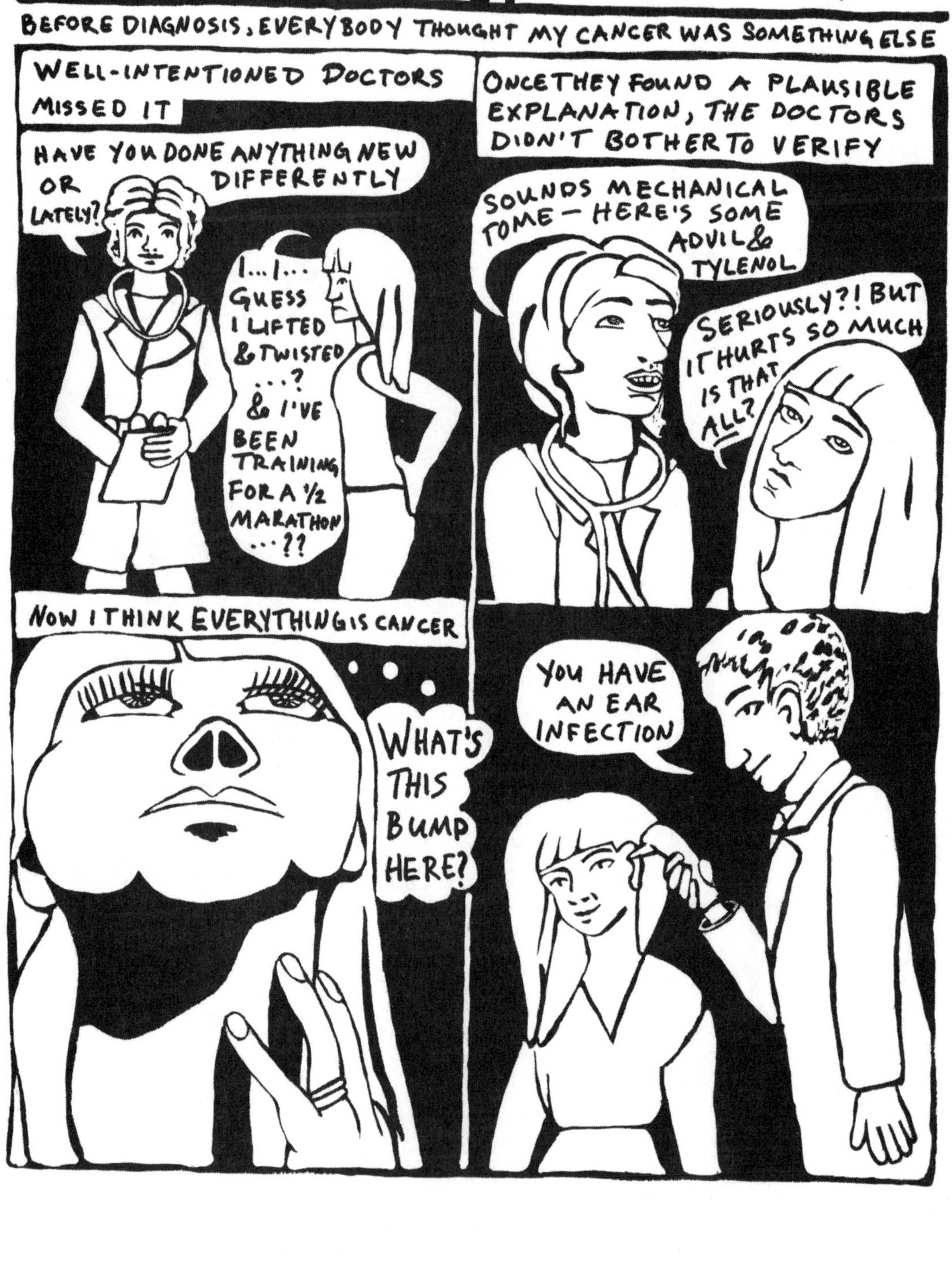

BEFORE DIAGNOSIS, EVERYBODY THOUGHT MY CANCER WAS SOMETHING ELSE
WELL-INTENTIONED DOCTORS MISSED IT
HAVE YOU DONE ANYTHING NEW OR DIFFERENTLY LATELY?
I... I... GUESS I LIFTED & TWISTED ...? & I'VE BEEN TRAINING FOR A ½ MARATHON ...??
ONCE THEY FOUND A PLAUSIBLE EXPLANATION, THE DOCTORS DIDN'T BOTHER TO VERIFY
SOUNDS MECHANICAL TO ME — HERE'S SOME ADVIL & TYLENOL
SERIOUSLY?! BUT IT HURTS SO MUCH IS THAT ALL?
NOW I THINK EVERYTHING IS CANCER
WHAT'S THIS BUMP HERE?
YOU HAVE AN EAR INFECTION

What's Wrong with Me?

I was in so much pain. All the time. Its onset was gradual, slippery. I'd wake up with hip pain. Carrying groceries was getting harder. I was training for my second half-marathon, and it was much harder than the first. I found that after a run, my back and hip ached. I thought this must be what aging felt like.

I asked my husband, "Is this normal?" but after a lifetime of soccer injuries, David's barometer wasn't calibrated normally.

So I tried to be stoic. I tried not to complain. I popped Advil and Tylenol, but they barely made a difference.

I had to speak at a conference. The drive was gruelling, stop-and-go traffic for hours. I grabbed my bag out of the back seat of the car, and with a casual twist of the back I was doubled over in pain. Confused and tired, I checked into my hotel room and lowered myself onto the bed. I popped some more painkillers and went to sleep. I had to speak at eight the next morning.

When I woke up, the pain was manageable again, so I spoke and drove home.

The next night, I was cooking dinner for friends. I reached for a hanging cast-iron pan, twisting again to set it on the burner. Pain shot through my back and I fell to the floor. I couldn't stand, so my husband cooked while I gave him directions. I took painkillers and a muscle relaxant with a glass of wine. By the time our guests arrived, I could stand but I couldn't sit, so we had dinner at the breakfast bar, with me forgoing the high stool.

I joked about injuries of age, how lifting and twisting was now a hazard for me.

After a fitful attempt at sleep, I woke my husband up to take me to emergency. The pain was excruciating.

When a doctor finally saw me, she asked about the circumstances, but she didn't send me for any tests. It seemed very clear to her that I had hurt myself mechanically. She gave me a prescription for codeine and sent me home to rest.

Back at work on Monday, I couldn't sit at my desk for more than a few minutes. The IT team rigged me a temporary standing desk by putting my computer on Styrofoam risers. I stood at the back of the boardroom during meetings. I kept trying to run, but it was becoming too painful to train. Since I was fundraising for the Nature Conservancy of Canada, I felt guilty about not completing the race. I felt as though I would be letting down everybody who donated to support me.

Months passed. Eventually, I gave up. Tears welling in my eyes, I asked my husband to run in my place.

TWO MONTHS LATER, I found a lump in my breast. It seemed to come out of nowhere, and it was huge. It was growing so quickly that it hurt. I went to my family doctor, and he told me that I shouldn't worry because cancer doesn't hurt. It was probably an infected duct, but he'd send me for an ultrasound just in case.

The ultrasound technician was jovial and pleasant, cracking jokes with me... until she wasn't. Sliding her cold implement over the jelly on my skin, she became very serious. That's when I knew, but I was still in denial.

It took ten very long days for the results to come back. When they did, my family doctor called me at my office and asked if I could come in right away. If I hadn't known before, I surely should have then. I was shaking when I told my boss that I had to go.

I don't think my doctor, who was very young, had ever been in the position to tell somebody that they may have cancer. He was gentle and serious. He had called ahead to the closest hospital to make sure that I could be seen for a mammogram. It was December and half the staff was gone, but they squeezed me in.

First, I had a mammogram. This technician had an even worse poker face than the last. She gave me a big concerned hug as I left the room. Based on the results, they sent me across the hall for a biopsy.

I had to wait another week for the results. On my way to the hospital, standing on the subway platform, I almost turned and ran the other way. I felt sick to my stomach. When I arrived, the doctor asked me if there was somebody who could come and be with me. I called my husband and he rushed in to hold my hand.

The doctor told me that I had stage III breast cancer, with lymph node involvement. He said that I would have to have chemo, then surgery, then radiation. He said that by this time next year, I'd be on the other side of it.

He drew me a timeline.

Then they sent me for a routine bone scan. That's when I learned the cancer had been in my bones all along. And that's when I learned that my cancer was already stage IV — incurable — that I would never be on the other side of it, that I would be in treatment for the rest of my life, and the odds were against my seeing old age.

It was December. David and I scrapped our holiday letter. We toyed with the idea of not telling anybody until January, so our friends and family could enjoy the holidays. We clung to each other while we cried. A nurse told me that everything tastes terrible during chemo, so we went on a grand tour of Toronto's newest restaurants. We opened our best bottle of wine and drank to now, to living.

I started treatment on New Year's Eve.

NOW CANCER IS making me a hypochondriac.

My hands are always scanning my body for change. Any bump is a new metastasized tumour until I am sure that it isn't. I live in dread of inevitable disease progression. I am just now learning to cope with the side effects of my current treatment, and every time the disease progresses my treatment will change. That is, until the treatments run dry.

I am so tired of having cancer. I am worn out by the anxiety, by the constant vigilance. I mean, I intend to live a really long time, but it makes me tired to think that I will be living with cancer forever.

And every time a bump isn't cancer, I feel my spent body unfurl, letting all the fatigue tumble out like so many skittering insects, like a popped water balloon.

I Can Feel It In My Bones

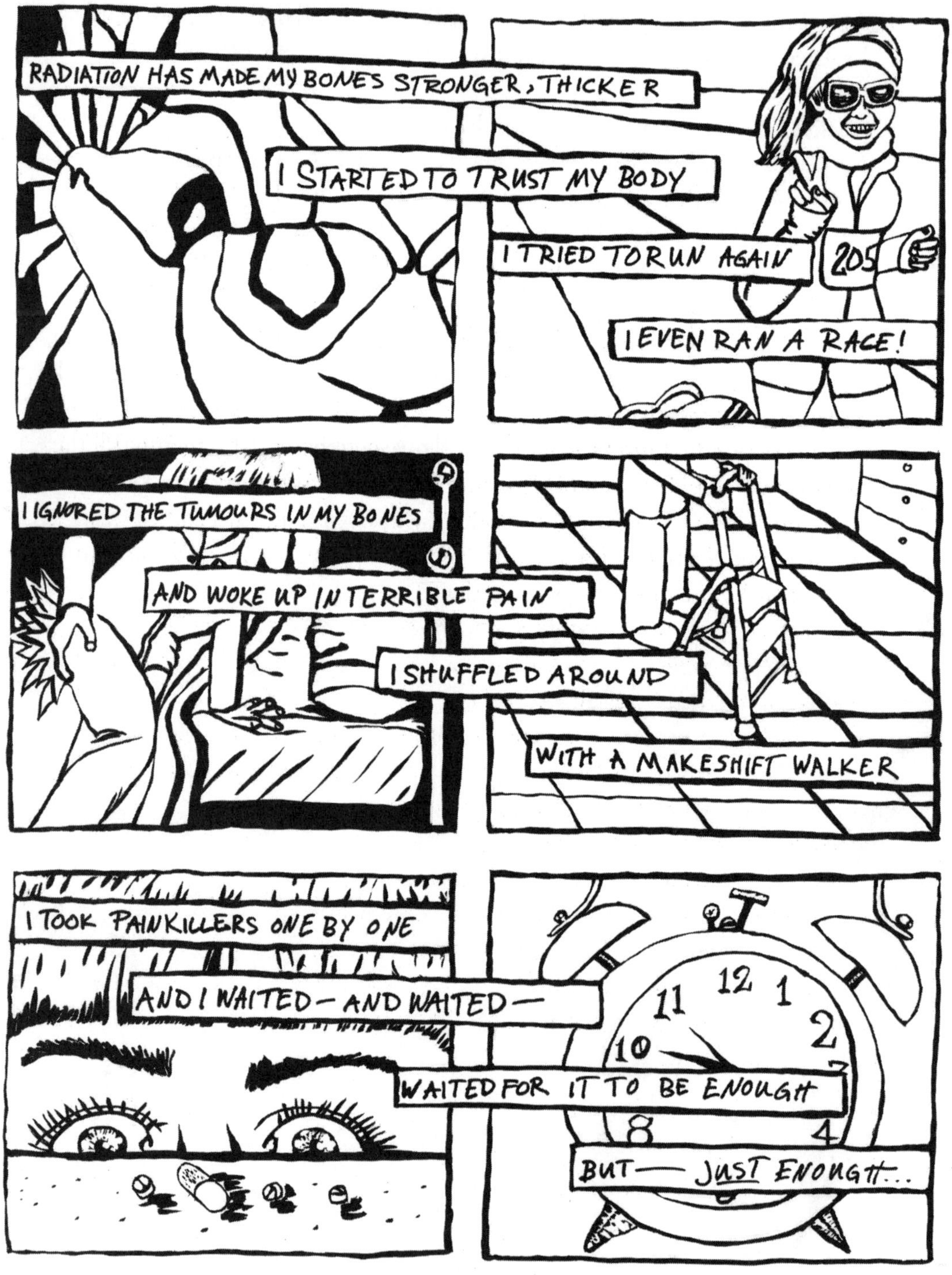

RADIATION HAS MADE MY BONES STRONGER, THICKER
I STARTED TO TRUST MY BODY
I TRIED TO RUN AGAIN
205
I EVEN RAN A RACE!
I IGNORED THE TUMOURS IN MY BONES
AND WOKE UP IN TERRIBLE PAIN
I SHUFFLED AROUND
WITH A MAKESHIFT WALKER
I TOOK PAINKILLERS ONE BY ONE
AND I WAITED — AND WAITED —
WAITED FOR IT TO BE ENOUGH
BUT — JUST ENOUGH...

I Can Feel It In My Bones

When I got sick, I felt it first in my bones, in my back. I'd find, one by one, things I could no longer do. I used to love road trips, but I couldn't bear to sit in the car for very long. I couldn't carry the laundry down two flights of stairs. I couldn't sleep comfortably, so I took pills. I couldn't have sex with my husband, so he held me while I cried. I couldn't lift and twist and carry things, so my husband helped me more and I got a pull cart for groceries.

Then I was diagnosed, and they gave me palliative radiation for the metastatic tumours (known as *mets*) in my bones. Angels sang. I could do things again. I felt especially lucky when I was cleared to run again.

So I signed up for a little run, just 8k, with a couple of friends, and we trained gently. But I could feel my body wanting to pull away, to pound the streets so I could feel that adrenaline course through me.

So race day, I let myself let go.

It felt delicious and verboten, like Eve's apple.

For the time that I was running, it felt like freedom.

Then, after, even though my bones were stronger because of radiation, they ached, dully and deeply. I couldn't get comfortable for days.

I have had to accept that that glorious feeling of freedom will have to come from somewhere new.

Some People Get Lucky

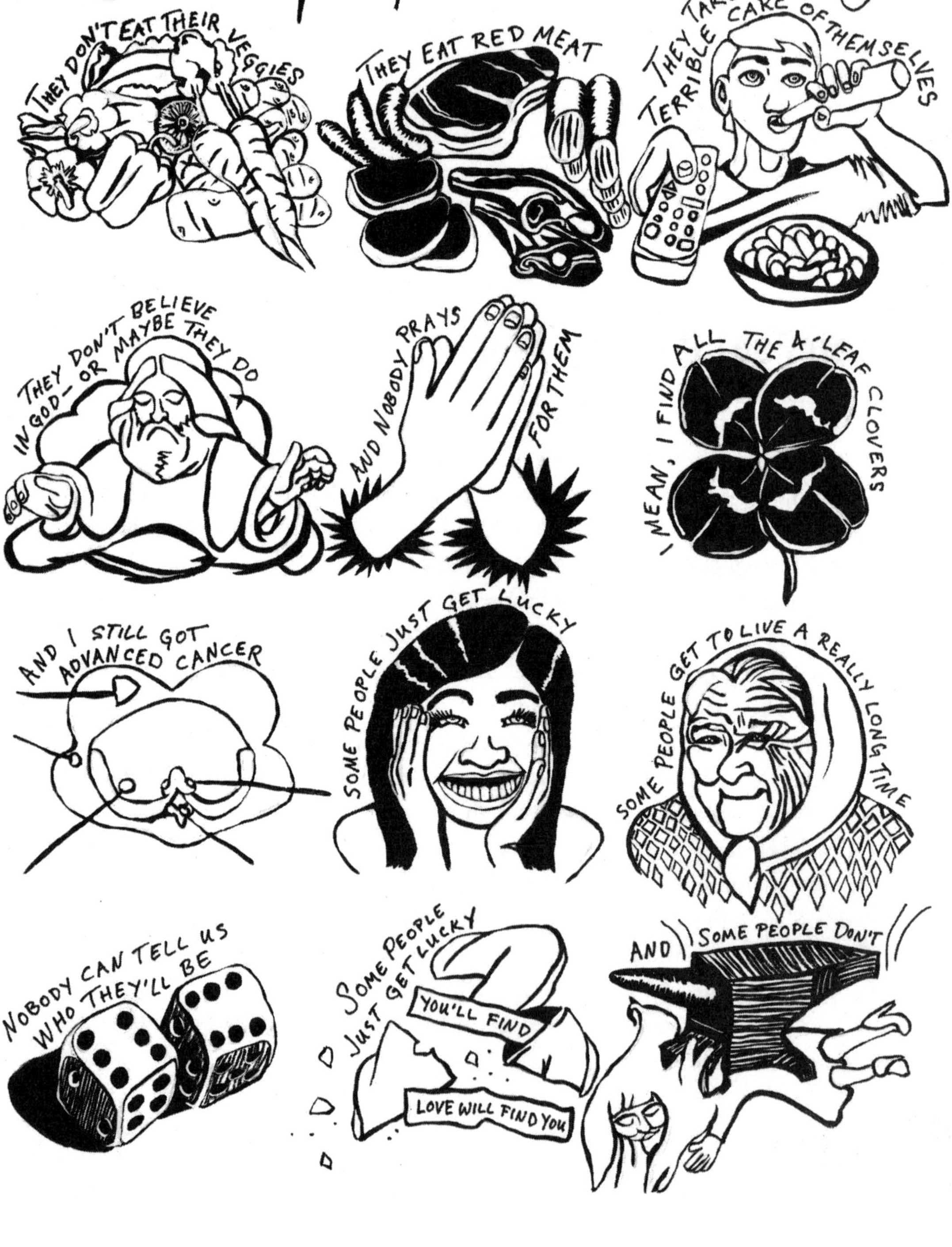

Some People Get Lucky

When I was first diagnosed, I made all these frantic lifestyle changes, as if I could turn back time, undo my bad luck. I think a lot of us do that.

You see, I wasn't always exactly a saint. From partying to salty chips, to working too long at a desk, to my on-again-off-again relationship with exercise—opportunities for self-blame were easy to find. I didn't even have to try. They crowded in, then squished in some more, like commuters on a Tokyo subway.

Too little too late, maybe, but I saw my diagnosis as an opportunity for improvement. I was already a vegetarian, so I became a vegan. I cut out all sugars, except those in fruits and vegetables. I juiced and drank murky, complicated smoothies. I spent hours scanning the Internet, looking into the efficacy of complementary therapies. I read pages and pages to make sure certain therapies weren't clearly hoaxes or actually dangerous, then I adopted everything that showed any conceivable promise: coriolus, reishi, and maitake mushrooms; turmeric; medical marijuana; frankincense; selenium; iodine; flaxseed oil—the list goes on and on. I checked every new supplement diligently with my hospital pharmacist to ensure that it wouldn't negate my oncologist's treatment. I took up swimming, since bone mets made running difficult; I practiced yoga regularly; I meditated.

I was frantic, driven by panic. I was trying to take some agency over my body. I told myself that it might not help, but it couldn't hurt. At least I'd be boosting my immune system. Giving my body its best chance. Making myself strong enough to withstand treatments. My oncologist shook his head, told me to stop wasting my money.

I did stop getting colds, but eventually the cancer progressed and my treatment changed.

IF I FOUND a magical elixir to turn back time, when would I go back to? What difference would it make, really, since my cancer is hereditary? Conception? Would I let the egg that became me flow, infertile, away with the menses?

No. I like to exist.

The clinical trial I'm on now doesn't allow most of the complementary therapies I was taking. We just don't know how they'll react with the investigational drug. So I eased off. I still take very good care of myself, but two years in, the fever pitch has slowed.

I mean, the cancer is here, and I have a life to live. And sometimes living well includes eating something made with sugar or having a glass of wine with dinner. I'm not going to be hard on myself. I'm going to enjoy every minute I can.

Plenty of people eat fast food every day, watch hours and hours of TV, get blackout drunk, and they're just fine. But it doesn't matter if I treat my body like a temple; the problem is in my genes.

So. Here I stand.

This is luck of the worst kind.

Great Expectations

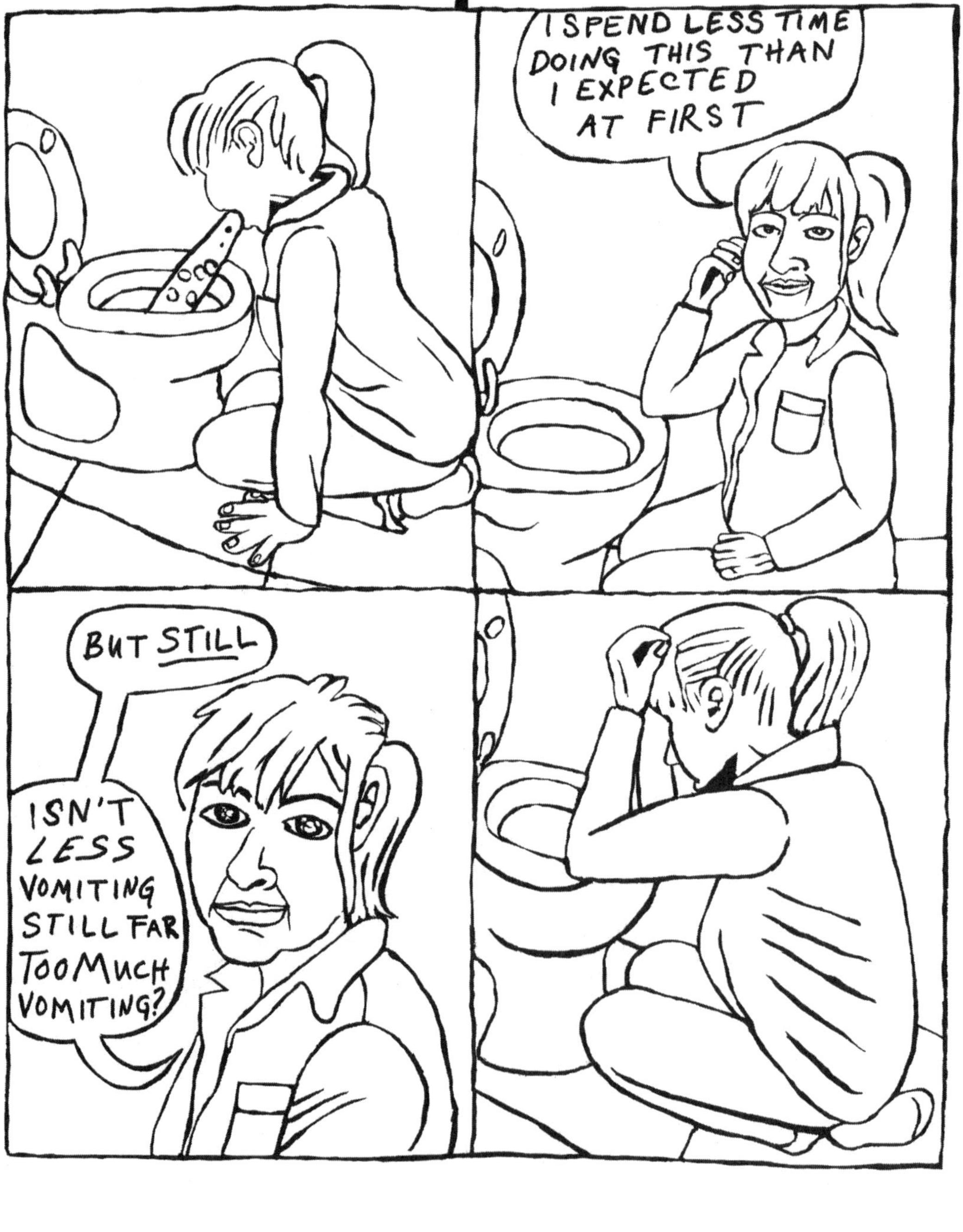
I SPEND LESS TIME DOING THIS THAN I EXPECTED AT FIRST
BUT STILL
ISN'T LESS VOMITING STILL FAR TOO MUCH VOMITING?

Great Expectations

Besides the loss of hair, this is what we think of when we think of cancer.

Hours spent on the bathroom floor, nothing left to give.

The reality is that antiemetics are pretty good these days. Most of the time, although we can't stop the nausea, we can stop the vomiting.

Most of the time.

So I don't spend nearly as much time like this as I expected.

But I spend enough time here that I've learned to keep hair elastics and a glass of water on hand all the time, and a new toothbrush as a reward when it's all over.

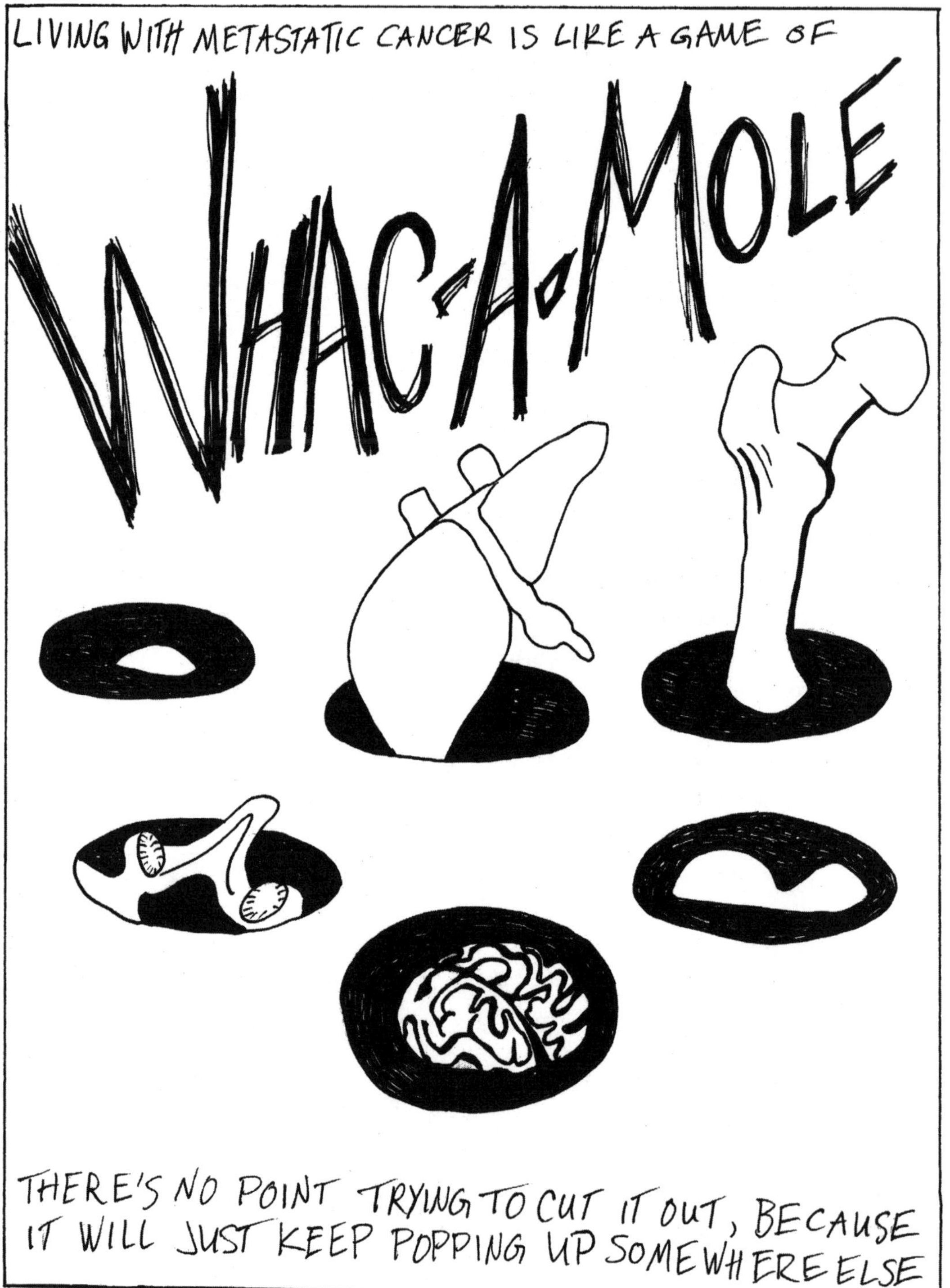
LIVING WITH METASTATIC CANCER IS LIKE A GAME OF
WHAC-A-MOLE
THERE'S NO POINT TRYING TO CUT IT OUT, BECAUSE IT WILL JUST KEEP POPPING UP SOMEWHERE ELSE

Whac-A-Mole: A Game of Mets

Living with out-of-the-gate metastatic cancer is different. Different than life before and different than I would have expected breast cancer to be, experientially.

You see, breast cancer has a powerful marketing machine that teaches us that diagnosis will occur in time for a cure. That cure will be comprised of chemo, surgery, radiation, and possibly an additional hormone therapy, depending on the profile of your cancer.

But when your cancer has already metastasized to remote parts of your body, by the time it's identified, you learn a different story. You learn that the horse has jumped the gate, so to speak; the cancer is already in your bones. Then you hear the chilling words, "We are no longer looking for a cure."

Only then do you learn that treatment is completely different. Because the doctors have no idea where your cancer might pop up next, they don't put your body through the trauma of surgery to remove what's already there.

Instead, treatment is systemic and palliative. The oncologists attempt to keep the cancer from spreading any more while trying to help you be as comfortable as possible. If you're lucky (as I am) and your cancer is estrogen positive, or fuelled by estrogen, they try to starve it with an oophorectomy or ovarian ablation and an estrogen-suppressing drug, kicking you into early, possibly permanent, menopause. Unlike chemo, this treatment leaves the rest of the body relatively unscathed. Hair doesn't fall out (at least not all of it). Skin doesn't get raw and cracked (although it gets dry and papery). Pain is treated with local radiation and opiates. And the doctors try to keep your quality of life up, prolonging the time you have before your body is ravaged by chemo.

Some women last a really long time on these kinds of treatments. And as much as cancer laughs in the face of my plans, I intend to be one of those women.

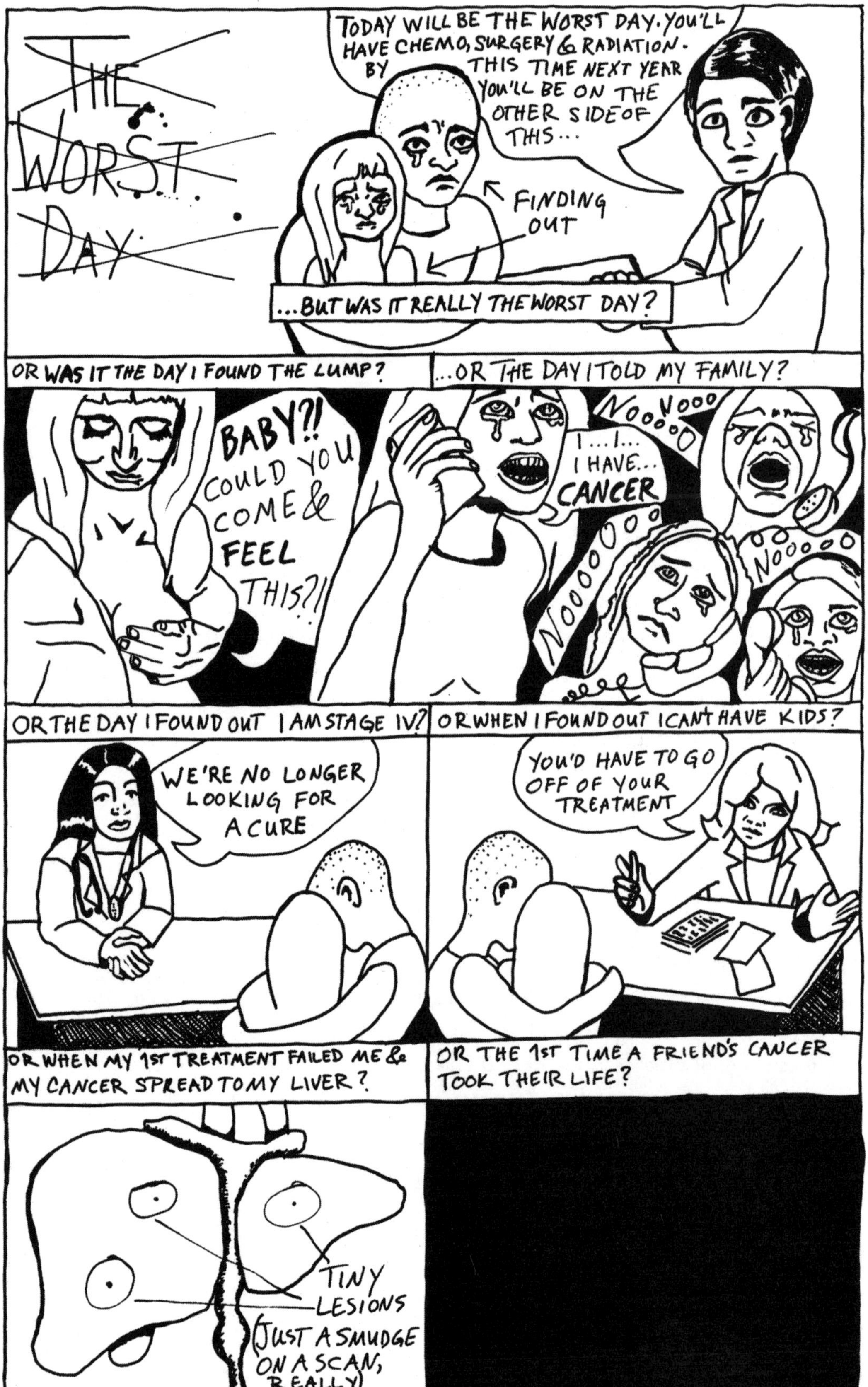
THE WORST DAY
TODAY WILL BE THE WORST DAY. YOU'LL HAVE CHEMO, SURGERY & RADIATION. BY THIS TIME NEXT YEAR YOU'LL BE ON THE OTHER SIDE OF THIS...
FINDING OUT
...BUT WAS IT REALLY THE WORST DAY?
OR WAS IT THE DAY I FOUND THE LUMP?
BABY?! COULD YOU COME & FEEL THIS?!
...OR THE DAY I TOLD MY FAMILY?
I...I... I HAVE... CANCER
NoooOooo
NooooOooo
Nooooo
OR THE DAY I FOUND OUT I AM STAGE IV?
WE'RE NO LONGER LOOKING FOR A CURE
OR WHEN I FOUND OUT I CAN'T HAVE KIDS?
YOU'D HAVE TO GO OFF OF YOUR TREATMENT
OR WHEN MY 1ST TREATMENT FAILED ME & MY CANCER SPREAD TO MY LIVER?
TINY LESIONS
(JUST A SMUDGE ON A SCAN, REALLY)
OR THE 1ST TIME A FRIEND'S CANCER TOOK THEIR LIFE?

The Worst Day

I'm finding the worst day to be a moving target. I mean, so is the best day, so it only makes sense. It's just that the extremes are more life or death.

Yet somehow, no matter how bad a day, I always find myself still standing. And even though I should add a qualifier like *so far*, I don't want to. Now is what I have and if I can get through the worst days, then I have earned the best days.

Cancer Fraud

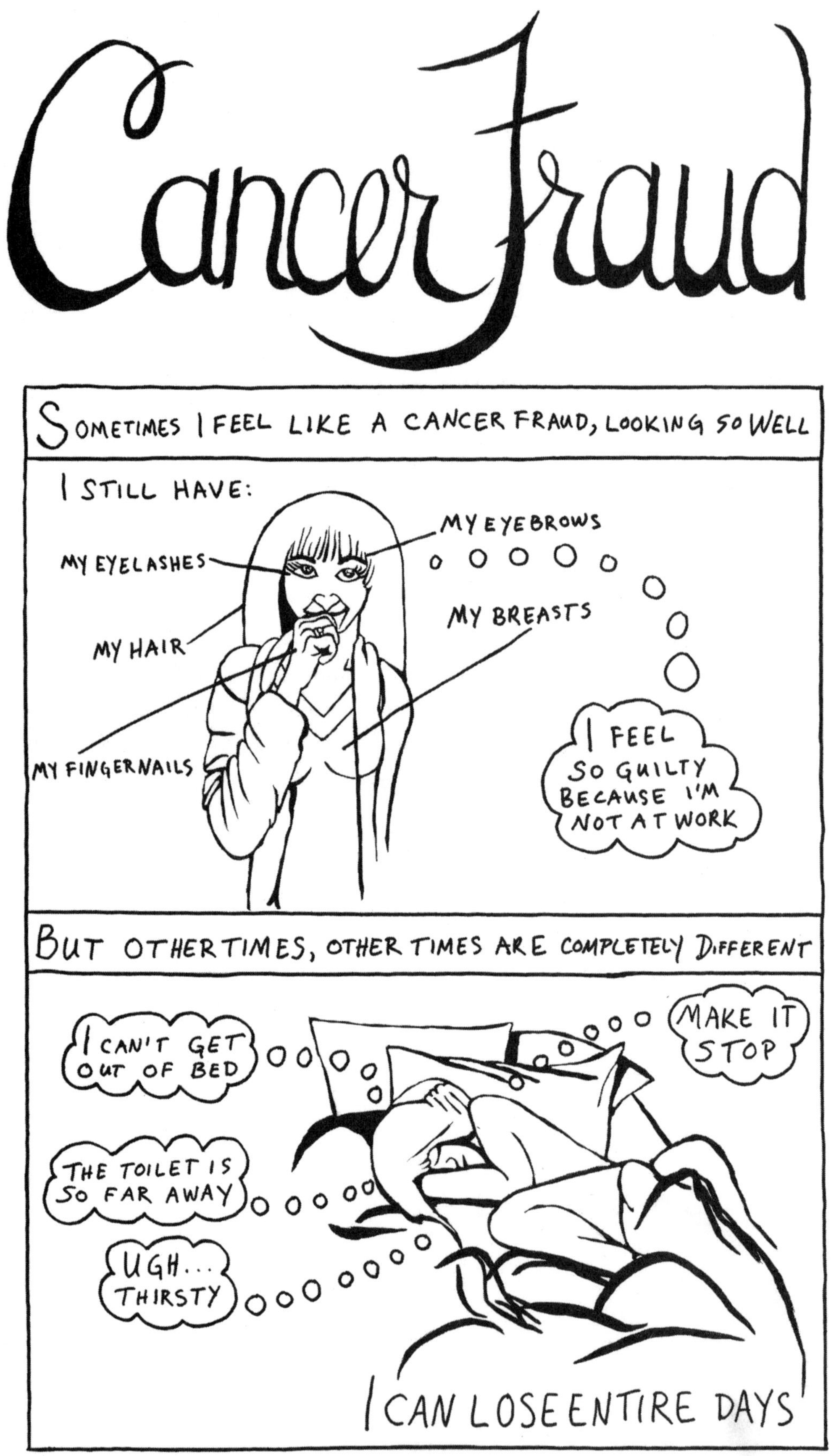

Sometimes I feel like a cancer fraud, looking so well
I still have:
My eyebrows
My eyelashes
My hair
My breasts
My fingernails
I feel so guilty because I'm not at work
But other times, other times are completely different
I can't get out of bed
Make it stop
The toilet is so far away
Ugh... thirsty
I can lose entire days

Cancer Fraud

Looks can be misleading with metastatic breast cancer. I can look so normal as to disappear. I could be any woman pushing forty but acting a lot younger. When I feel well, when my pain management is just so, when I've been able to sleep, when I've been away from the hospital for a few days, it's almost as if I am, in fact, well. For a minute, or a day, or maybe even longer.

And when I feel well, I try to live my life like a well person. I leave the house. I do my own grocery shopping. I ride my bike around town. I pop in and out of stores, seeing what's changed since I last visited. I see my friends, and sometimes I don't even ask them to come to me. I take care of things that have been nagging at me, like tackling that pile of paper that insists on accumulating: bills mixed in with sweet letters I'll save and paperwork from the hospital. I might even go out late to see a band. I might dance. I might even nurse one glass of wine all night. Then I really look normal.

But there's a trick to this. I can keep feeling well longer if I'm choosy. I can't do all the things, even on my best days. So I make lists and I rank things. I ask myself how much energy I really have. If I ride my bike, will I have to give up making a nice dinner for my husband? If I stay up late to see a favourite band play, will I be able to get out of bed to draw in the morning, or will I sleep the day away?

And it changes. Just because I think I feel well enough doesn't mean that I am. I might show up full of hope and then need to make a hasty exit before the evening's main event.

Yet on the days when I feel strong and able, I wonder what I'm doing. I wonder why I'm not back at work, doing the job I love. And on the days when I feel well,

I miss it so much it hurts. I feel like a fraud, because in that moment, I feel able to go back to my old life.

Other days are different. Other days, when I can't get out of bed, I don't feel like a fraud. These are the days when it hurts to lie in any position. I squirm and contort, trying to wriggle away from the pain, from the ache that's in my bones and the muscles that support them. I build a nest of pillows to support my wretched body. Or I'm too tired even to squirm. I sleep strange hours, drifting in and out of pain. Every time I wake up, I am parched. Sometimes I slide along the wall to the bathroom, too weak to walk without support. I have to pee for long minutes. Then I stagger to the kitchen and make myself chew and swallow a rice cake.

Some days, I camp out at the hospital with my "go" bag, which carries water, books, snacks, and a blanket. Hours disappear. I give blood with one arm and get an injection in the other, then another in my stomach. I am weighed and measured; my symptoms are documented meticulously. These are the days when I can't pretend for a second that it's not real. These are the days that I wish I were a fraud.

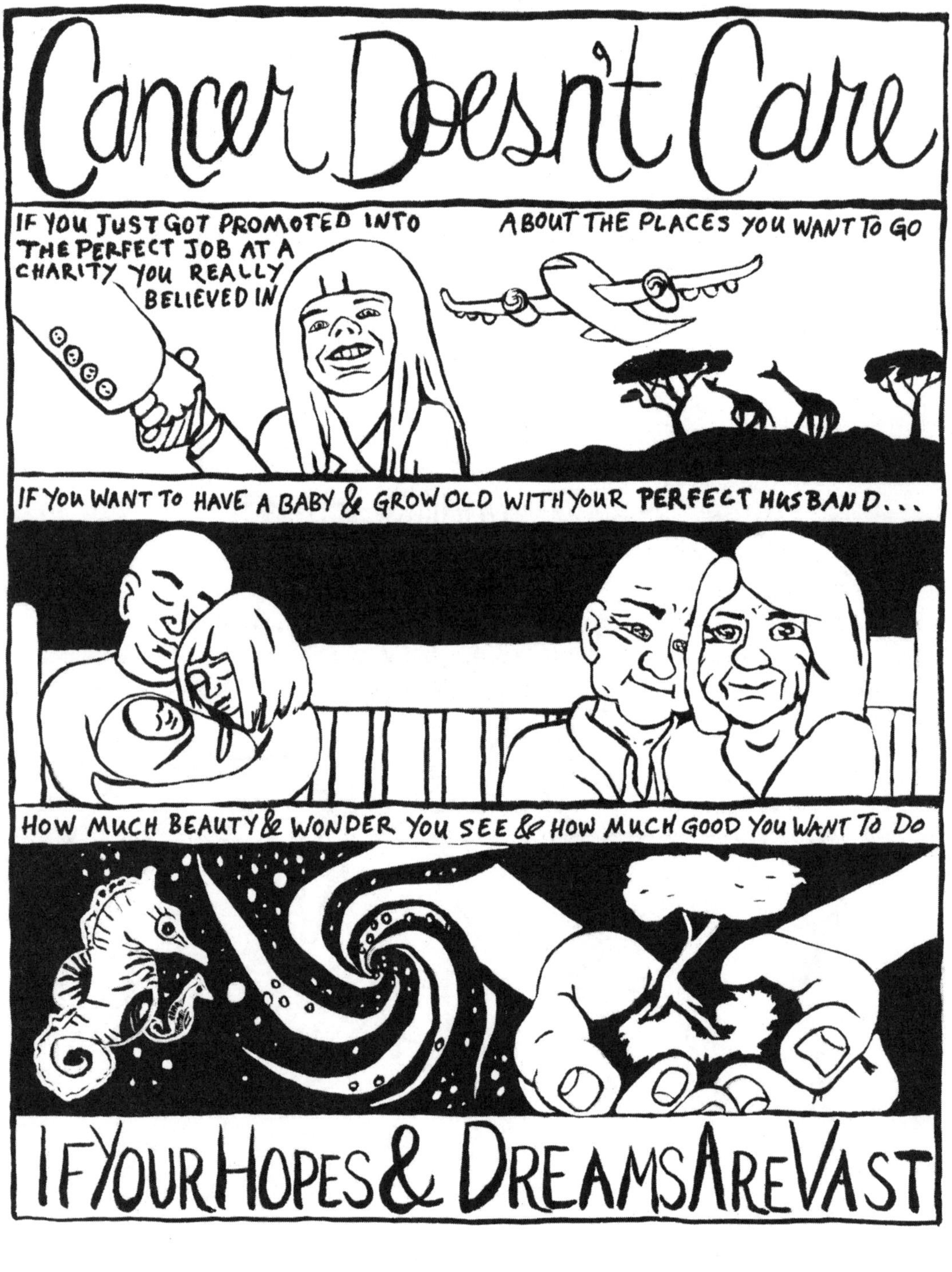
Cancer Doesn't Care
IF YOU JUST GOT PROMOTED INTO THE PERFECT JOB AT A CHARITY YOU REALLY BELIEVED IN
ABOUT THE PLACES YOU WANT TO GO
IF YOU WANT TO HAVE A BABY & GROW OLD WITH YOUR PERFECT HUSBAND...
HOW MUCH BEAUTY & WONDER YOU SEE & HOW MUCH GOOD YOU WANT TO DO
IF YOUR HOPES & DREAMS ARE VAST

Cancer Doesn't Care

We have a deep need to attribute a personality to cancer.

But there's no inherent animosity, just as there's no inherent kindness.

Cancer isn't a person that cares.

And having cancer doesn't make me special. There are so many of us living with this multi-faceted disease. It feels random and unpredictable, but the odds were really against me: I was born into a high-risk family within the globally higher-risk population of Ashkenazi Jews.

But rather than focus on what cancer takes away, I try to focus on what it doesn't. Because as much as I've lost, my life is really rich and full. I have a remarkable love (truly, everybody remarks on it), a space to write and draw when I have energy, a warm and intelligent family, inspiring friends.

There is so much beauty in the world.

Treatment

BY THE SKIN OF MY TEETH

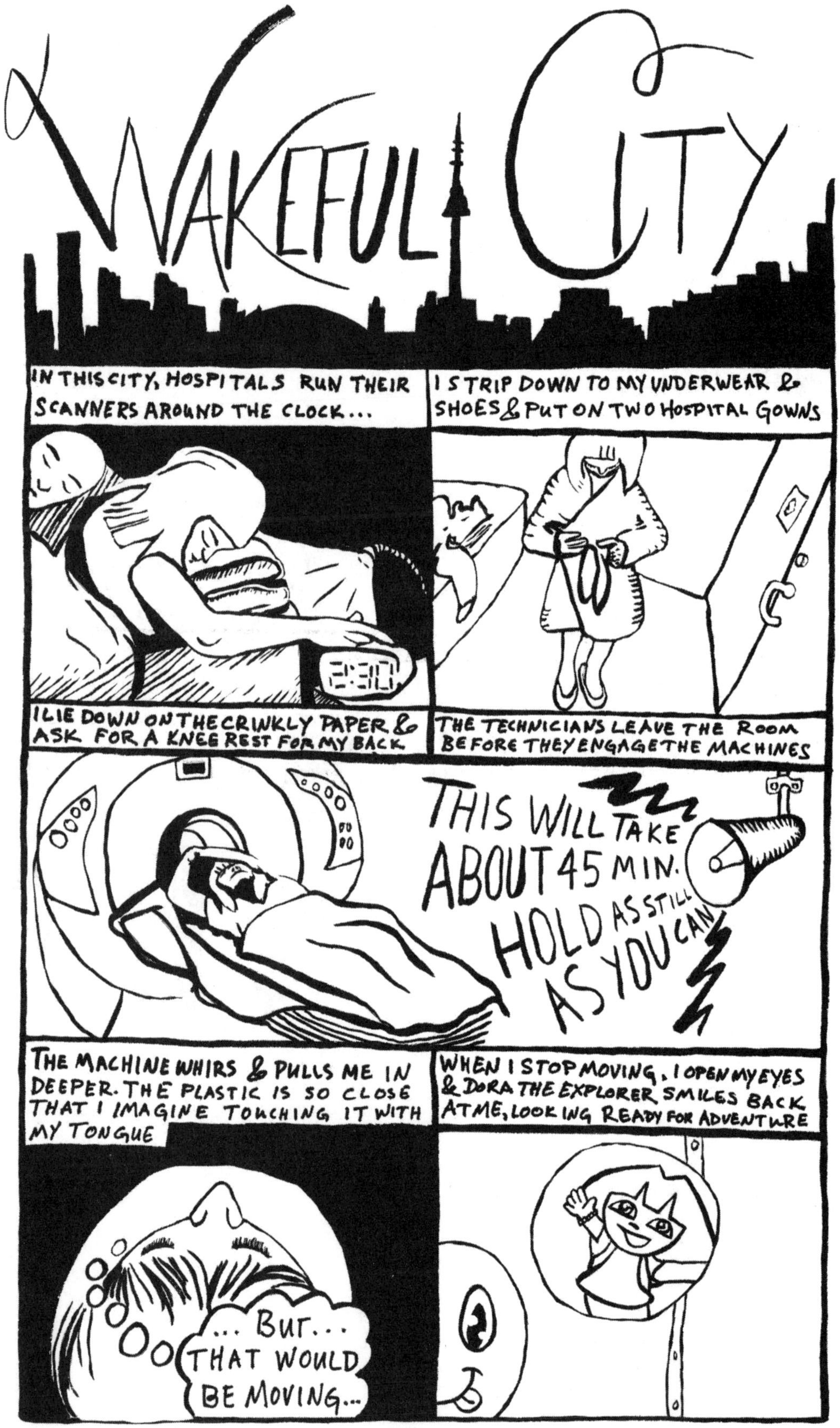
WAKEFUL CITY
IN THIS CITY, HOSPITALS RUN THEIR SCANNERS AROUND THE CLOCK...
I STRIP DOWN TO MY UNDERWEAR & SHOES & PUT ON TWO HOSPITAL GOWNS
I LIE DOWN ON THE CRINKLY PAPER & ASK FOR A KNEE REST FOR MY BACK
THE TECHNICIANS LEAVE THE ROOM BEFORE THEY ENGAGE THE MACHINES
THIS WILL TAKE ABOUT 45 MIN. HOLD AS STILL AS YOU CAN
THE MACHINE WHIRS & PULLS ME IN DEEPER. THE PLASTIC IS SO CLOSE THAT I IMAGINE TOUCHING IT WITH MY TONGUE
...BUT... THAT WOULD BE MOVING...
WHEN I STOP MOVING, I OPEN MY EYES & DORA THE EXPLORER SMILES BACK AT ME, LOOKING READY FOR ADVENTURE

Wakeful City

In this city, demand is so high that MRI machines run around the clock. With technicians on shift-work schedules, the timing is largely luck of the draw. And nobody draws the long straw every time.

I went in for an MRI at 3:45 a.m. There is no sleep schedule these appointments don't destroy.

At that hour, I enter through the chaos of emergency, and then walk, alone, through the echoing empty halls of the hospital.

When I reach the waiting room, instead of a receptionist, there's a laminated sign with a phone number propped by a phone on a small table. I call the number and wait. The overnight technician comes and leads me deeper into the hospital to fill out paperwork, take off any metal items, and change into a robe.

So still, so quiet.

As the machine pulls me in, I am struck by how much the whirring, ticking, clicking, and humming sounds like electronic music—spare breakcore or sometimes hard techno. But there's not a lot of room for dancing in the MRI machine. In fact, no moving is allowed.

I am getting very good at lying still.

When the bed stops moving, my eyes flutter open. Someone has put Dora the Explorer stickers on the ceiling. I picture how it must feel to be a kid in here, how scary and strange. My heart crumples.

I breathe. And with that breath, I smile a little, thinking that somebody at the hospital went room to room, reaching in and pasting stickers in the MRI machines to bring a spot of joy and familiarity into this sterile place for the kids being treated. And I focus on Dora, who smiles right back at me, ready for adventure.

On a Platter

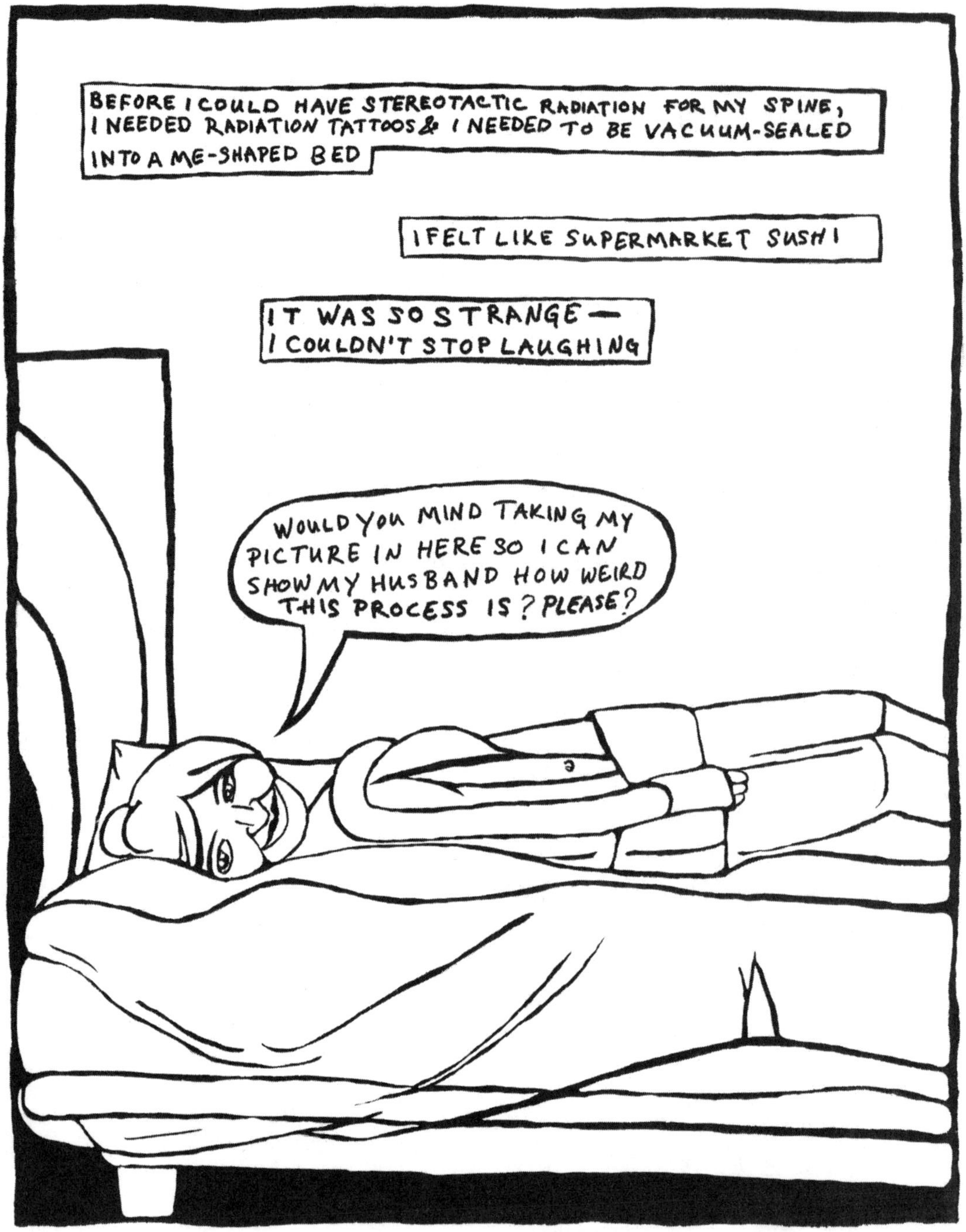
BEFORE I COULD HAVE STEREOTACTIC RADIATION FOR MY SPINE, I NEEDED RADIATION TATTOOS & I NEEDED TO BE VACUUM-SEALED INTO A ME-SHAPED BED
I FELT LIKE SUPERMARKET SUSHI
IT WAS SO STRANGE — I COULDN'T STOP LAUGHING
WOULD YOU MIND TAKING MY PICTURE IN HERE SO I CAN SHOW MY HUSBAND HOW WEIRD THIS PROCESS IS? PLEASE?

On a Platter

Sometimes treatment takes a turn for the absurd. Like when you need very precise spinal stereotactic radiation therapy, and holding still just isn't good enough.

To prepare, I needed to be immobilized. I lay on a deflated mould that felt like a beanbag chair, contained by high walls. Technicians vacuumed all the air out of the mould, which hardened around my reclining body. As a guide for future positioning, they gave me tiny permanent tattoos. Finally I was shrink-wrapped in. This way, every day of treatment, they could put my body in the exact same position, which is important because they were delivering a very high dose of radiation that needed to go directly into my L1 vertebra, which has quite a nasty tumour. No wonder my back had been a disaster for years.

The process was so strange and new to me, I couldn't stop laughing. Having been wrapped up like a tray of sushi, I asked the technician to go into my purse, take out my phone, and take a picture of me so I could show my husband.

Everything about treatment would be so fascinating if it just weren't happening to me. It's as if I just wandered away from my life full of offices and meetings into a surrealist dream sequence — not all nightmare, but completely absurd.

As Bad As It Gets

I FOUND MYSELF IN ER, 2 WEEKS AWAY FROM SOLID FOOD, I WAS RAIL THIN, UNABLE EVEN TO KEEP FLUIDS OR MEDICATION DOWN

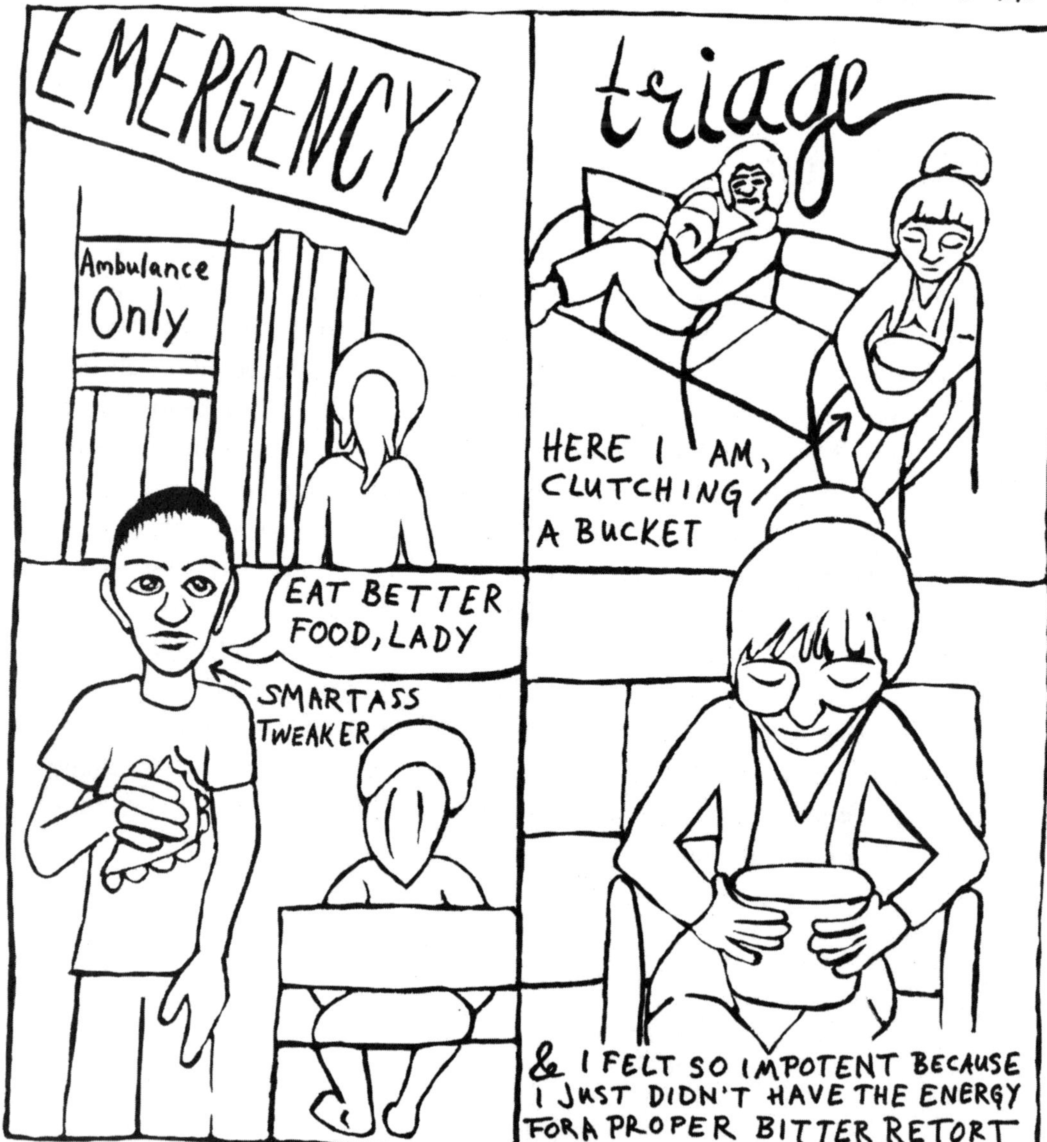
EMERGENCY
Ambulance Only
triage
HERE I AM, CLUTCHING A BUCKET
EAT BETTER FOOD, LADY
SMARTASS TWEAKER
& I FELT SO IMPOTENT BECAUSE I JUST DIDN'T HAVE THE ENERGY FOR A PROPER BITTER RETORT

As Bad As It Gets

When the vomiting started, I didn't know why. I threw everything I had at it—from ginger Gravol to Metoclopramide—but it all failed me. I eventually tried using medical marijuana to calm my stomach. Although it was incredibly effective against radiation-related emesis, pot only made this vomiting worse. I couldn't keep anything down, not even water, and the mere smell of food sent me running to the bathroom.

Like many people living with cancer, I manage pain with opiates. They're incredibly effective, and doctors like them because they have no ceiling, meaning that as pain increases, the dosage can be increased. Our bodies get used to most of the side effects, allowing us to live fairly well. I eventually stopped being drowsy, spacey, and floaty, but my bowels never learned to work around them.

Even though I take a research drug known to potentially cause diarrhea, I managed to get so constipated that food was doing a U-turn at my bowels and heading back the way it came. I knew that hydromorphone caused constipation, both theoretically and experientially, but I had no idea that it was possible to be dangerously constipated and to still have daily bowel movements.

Yet that's exactly what was happening to me, landing me in the emergency room.

My palliative care team put me on an aggressive laxative schedule and a liquid diet. In the short term, I needed to empty my bowels. Once that was done, I was to monitor my bowel movements and use whatever laxatives I needed to get myself on a pre-cancer bathroom schedule.

They also changed my opiate from a pill to a patch because the patch doesn't move the opiate through the stomach. Instead it absorbs the drugs through the skin and into the bloodstream, making the bowels less sluggish.

I went home feeling optimistic, but I hadn't eaten solid food for a week. My brain was foggy and slow.

When I got home, I pulled a sheet of stickers out of the box of patches, applied one, and went about my day.

Except that I couldn't go about my day because I was feeling worse. It had now been more than a week since I'd eaten solid food. The vomiting started again. My bowels liquefied. I broke out in full body sweats. I was writhing in bed, unable to sleep.

And that's how I ended up in emergency again, for the second time in as many weeks.

I'M THE KIND of person who talks back to the ranters on the street. When a scruffy man with bare feet and a wizard cloak cursed my family while standing on a trash can, I stopped in my tracks and argued with him, demanding that he take it back, that my family didn't deserve his curses.

But not this time. A sketchy guy was holding court in triage, waiting for his safe injection. He waved his hospital-issued sandwich in my face while he told me what to eat, and I just didn't have the force of will to tell him to go fuck himself.

It was all I could do to hold onto my bucket and hold myself together.

AT THIS POINT, nobody knew what was wrong with me. My most recent scans had shown no disease progression, but they hadn't included a brain scan. A CT scan done in emergency showed there was no mass large enough to be causing my symptoms, but a small metastasis could have been missed because the imaging team had used no contrast. Worried that my disease had crossed the blood-brain barrier, my oncologist ordered a brain MRI.

I'd been on a liquid diet for almost two weeks. I'd lost a lot of weight that I didn't really have to spare. Strangely, I was starting to feel a bit better. My brain was clearing up, and I was able to think more lucidly again.

When I went to put on my third three-day patch, I realized why. Because my brain function had been diminished by mild starvation, I did something I'd never have done were I in my right mind: I had applied the date-tracking stickers enclosed with the patch instead of the patch itself, plunging myself into full-blown opiate withdrawal.

It's no wonder the doctors had no idea what was wrong with me. They only knew what I'd told them, and I told them that I'd applied the patch. Learning that it was the drugs, not the disease, was a relief of epic proportion.

THE SYMPTOMS OF opiate withdrawal resemble the symptoms of a quite serious metastasis to the brain, which is one of the scariest monsters living in the shadows of my mind.

For me, living with metastatic breast cancer is living in fear. I am constantly waiting for the other shoe to drop. So are my doctors.

I report every change to my sleep, my energy, my bowel movements, my mood. It could all mean something huge, or it could all be nothing, but my doctors and nurses watch for patterns. I get embarrassed, feel a bit demoralized, but it could be a matter of life and death for me.

Even though I'm being treated with the most cutting-edge medicine, my disease can't be contained forever. And there's no schedule or formula for when it will leap onto the next organ, or start to grow where it's already ensconced. If a treatment works (and the treatments don't all work for everybody), it could work for weeks, months, or years.

We count in months the way parents count the age of babies. Eight months. Twelve months. Eighteen months. Only exceptional responders, who have rare long-lasting reprieves, seem to get to count in years.

My hopes are wrapped up in three-month increments, which is when I have the scans that tell me if I'm still stable.

WHAT I WANT

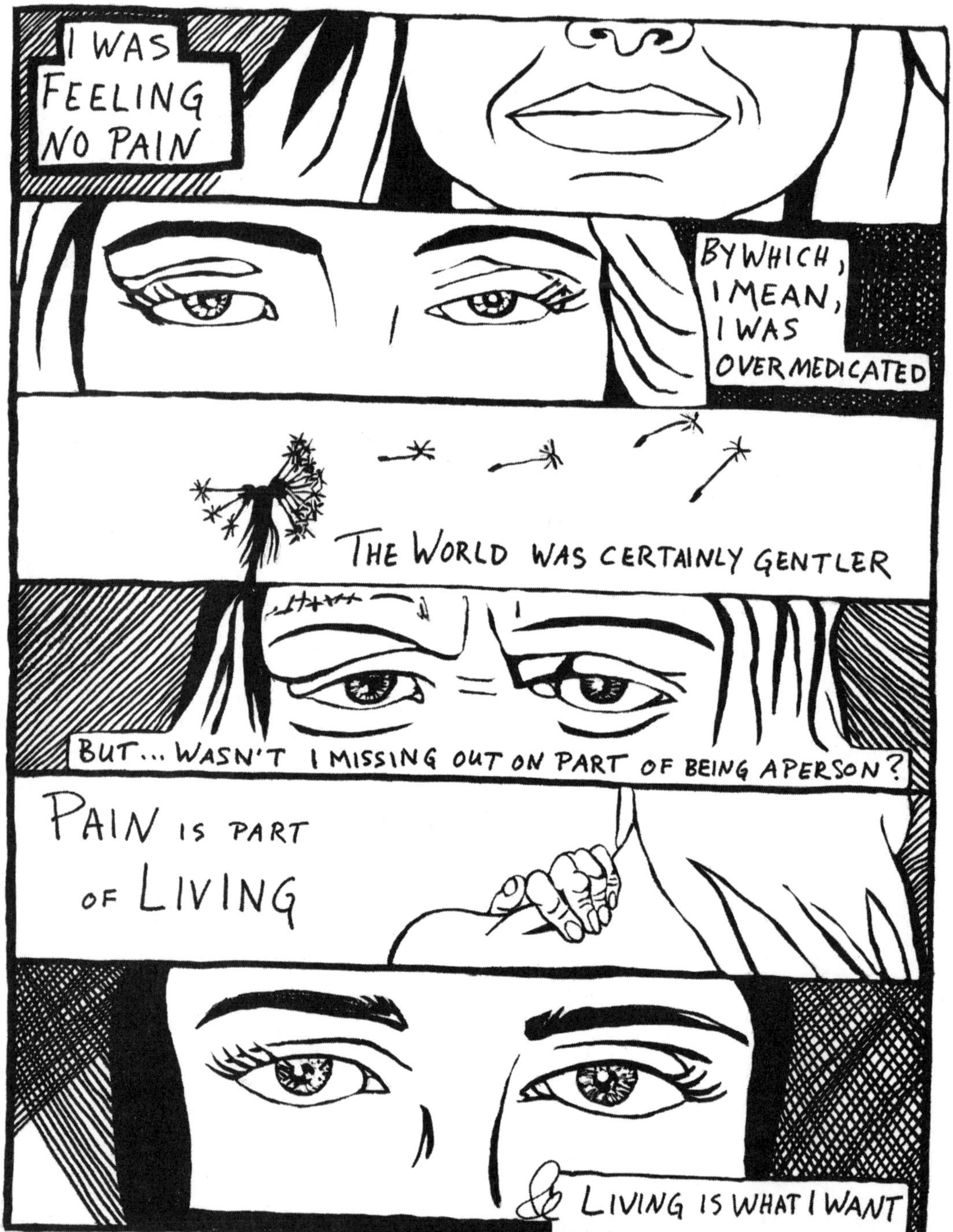

I WAS FEELING NO PAIN
BY WHICH, I MEAN, I WAS OVERMEDICATED
THE WORLD WAS CERTAINLY GENTLER
BUT... WASN'T I MISSING OUT ON PART OF BEING A PERSON?
PAIN IS PART OF LIVING
& LIVING IS WHAT I WANT

What I Want

A compassionate doctor told me that I shouldn't be feeling pain. I liked the sound of that, so I agreed. We raised my opiates accordingly.

Man, oh man, can I tell you? What a sweet thing to feel no pain, to simply be comfortable in my skin.

I mean, I'd forgotten how it felt to sit easily.

But there's a cost to everything, isn't there?

To live without pain, entirely, I'd have to live with my senses dulled. I'd have to slip into the soft cocoon of opiates and stay there.

I would miss so much of living.

Pain Management

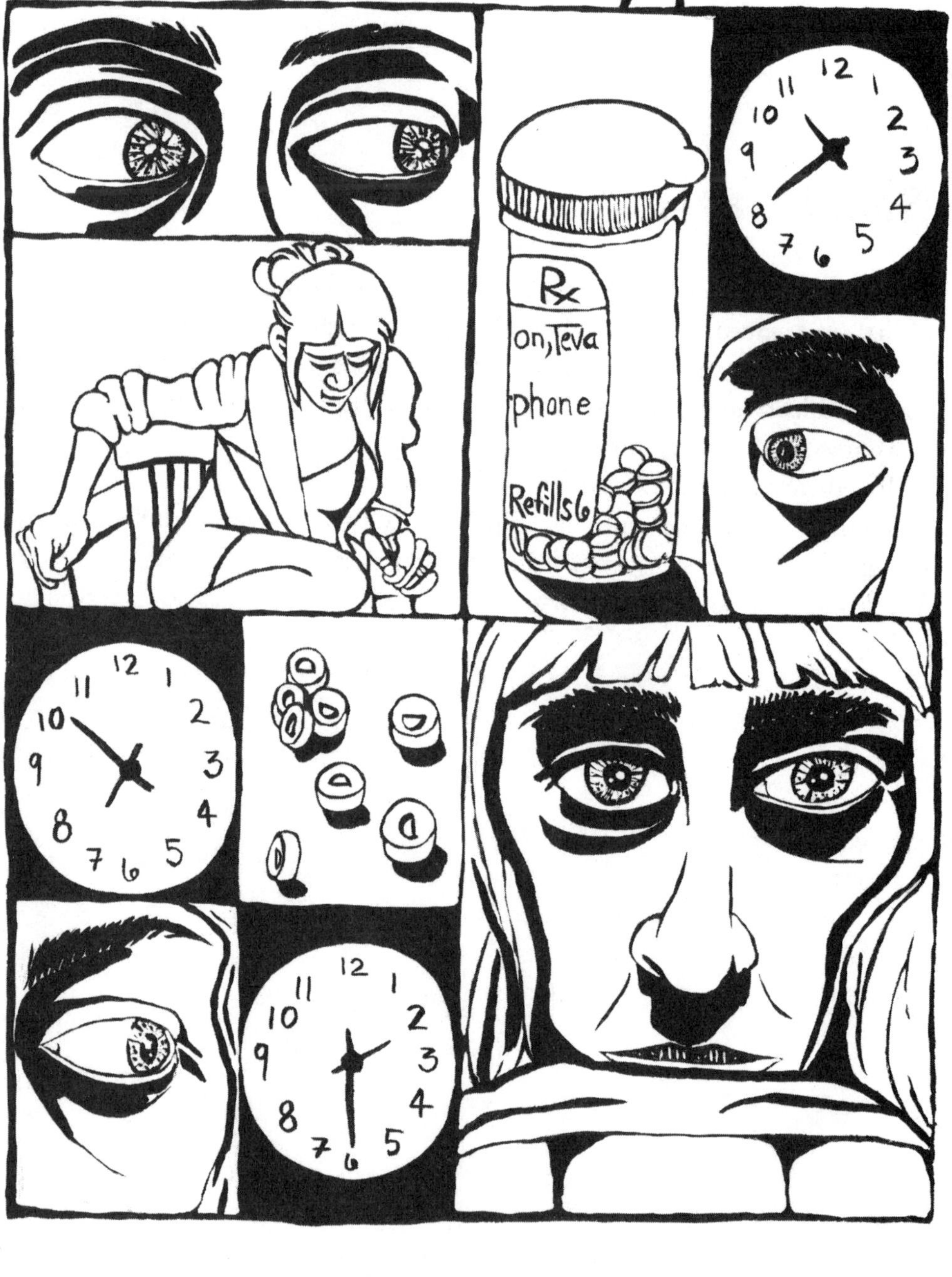
Rx
on,Teva
phone
Refills6

Pain Management

The pain pulses. It throbs. Sometimes it stabs.

The pain aches. It's in my bones. My muscles tense protectively.

It demands attention. Constant care and feeding.

And I have to be careful, because I manage it with narcotics, and narcotics are dangerous.

I take a baseline amount, a long-acting version, every day. I have to maintain a minimum level or the pain becomes unbearable.

And I always carry breakthroughs with me, in case of (get this literal name) breakthrough pain. I can only take one breakthrough per hour, except under exceptional circumstances. I can't make a habit of it. It takes an hour for them to come to full strength, so if I take them too soon, I could overdo it. I could make myself vague and floaty instead of sharp and clear.

Fuzzing my overactive brain is an attractive idea, sure, but a bad habit that I don't want to form. Because if I take too much, too often, my body will acclimate, and what was previously too much will become just enough.

Even as the pain persists, I wait. I watch the clock and rate my pain in my head. Is it bearable? Can I manage this much pain and go about my day?

And once an hour has passed, I just might have to do it all over again. So, the day has been spent watching clocks and measuring pain.

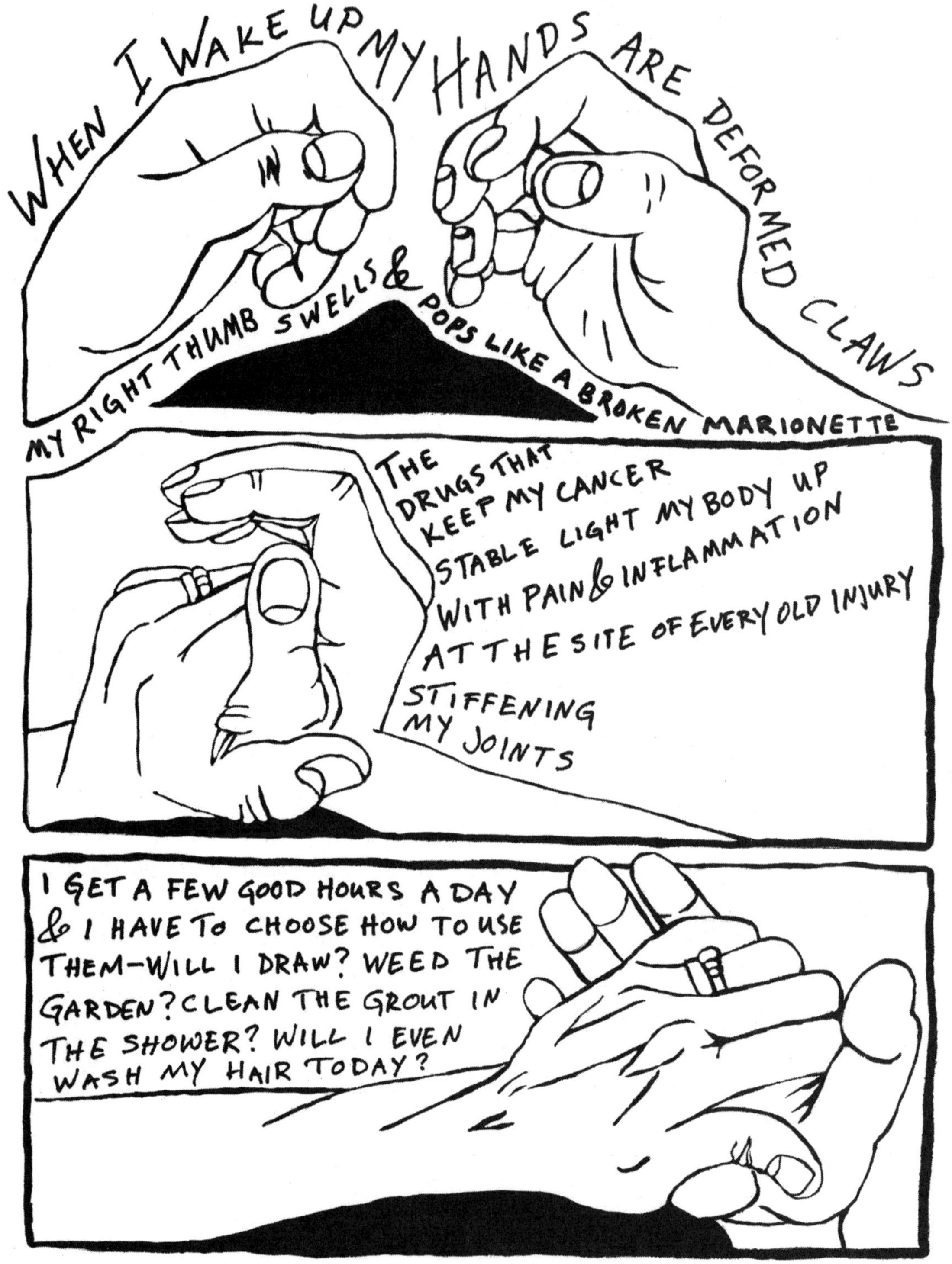
WHEN I WAKE UP MY HANDS ARE DEFORMED CLAWS
MY RIGHT THUMB SWELLS & POPS LIKE A BROKEN MARIONETTE
THE DRUGS THAT KEEP MY CANCER STABLE LIGHT MY BODY UP WITH PAIN & INFLAMMATION AT THE SITE OF EVERY OLD INJURY
STIFFENING MY JOINTS
I GET A FEW GOOD HOURS A DAY & I HAVE TO CHOOSE HOW TO USE THEM—WILL I DRAW? WEED THE GARDEN? CLEAN THE GROUT IN THE SHOWER? WILL I EVEN WASH MY HAIR TODAY?

When I Wake Up

The drugs I take are keeping my cancer stable, for now. That's what I care about. So what if they come with side effects specifically designed to torture me?

I love to make things with my hands. It's how I relate to the world around me. From cooking to sewing, painting to gardening, everything I most love doing requires my hands.

And some days, my hands don't work.

This forces me to slow down. Because my body needs to rest in order to be strong enough to fight the rogue cancer cells that are making their nihilistic way through my body.

But rest can be a torment on its own. When my body slows to nothing, oppressive white noise fills my head. A surging wall of anxiety washes over me, and I struggle to keep from going under.

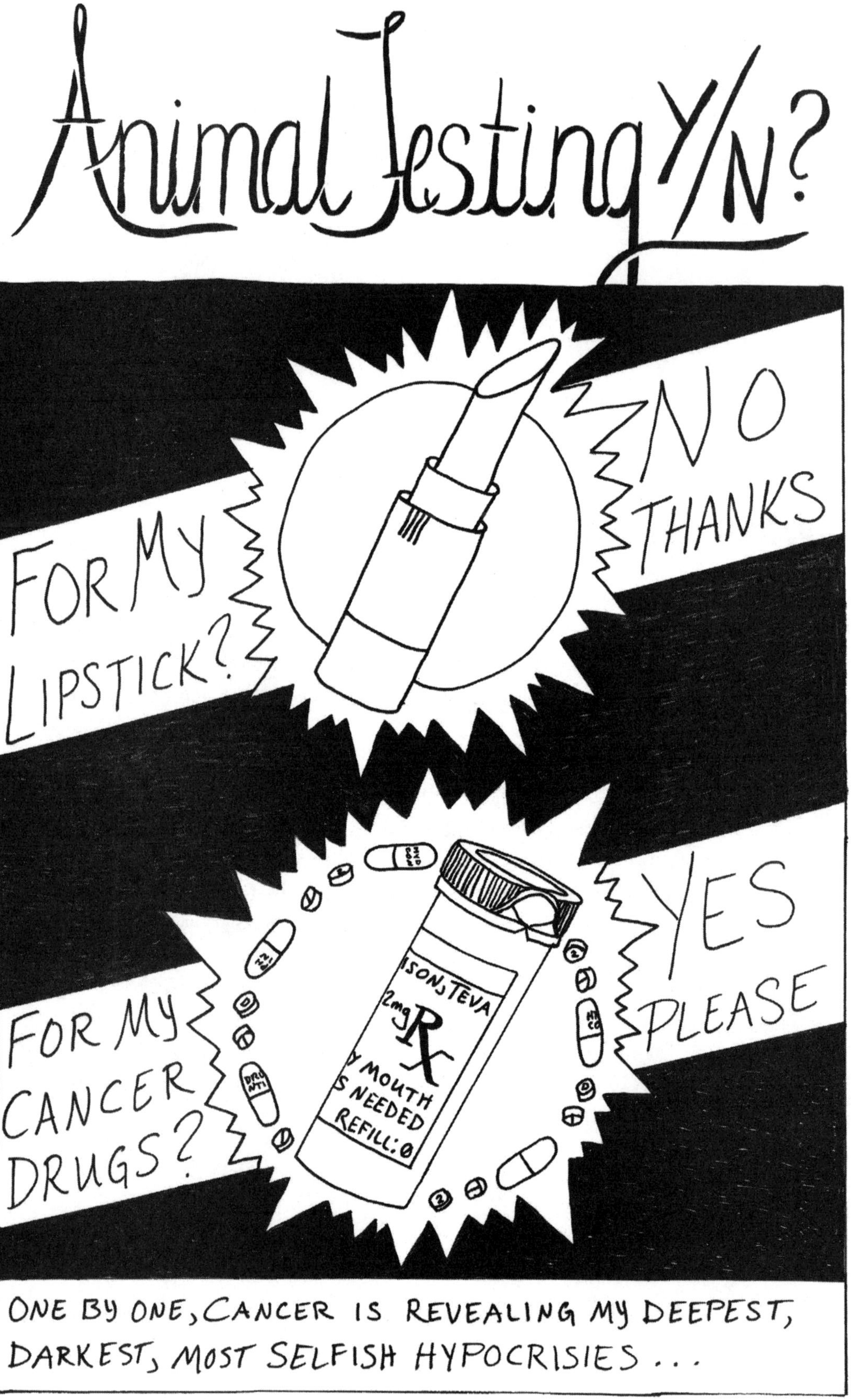
Animal Testing Y/N?
FOR MY LIPSTICK?
NO THANKS
FOR MY CANCER DRUGS?
ISON, TEVA
2mg
Rx
Y MOUTH
S NEEDED
REFILL: 0
YES PLEASE
ONE BY ONE, CANCER IS REVEALING MY DEEPEST, DARKEST, MOST SELFISH HYPOCRISIES . . .

Animal Testing Y/N

I've been a vegetarian my whole life, and I'm mostly vegan now. Add to that gluten, chickpea, and cucumber sensitivities, and I'm a nightmare for anybody else to feed.

I have been against animal testing for as long as I can remember. I love animals, and I don't think that my life is any more valuable than theirs.

Or do I?

Because now that I am part of a clinical trial, I am grateful that the investigational drug I'm taking was tested in vivo before being tested on me. I was okay with it even before I learned that those test subjects were likely cats and dogs with feline or canine breast cancers, animals who might have benefitted from the treatment.

And I'm grateful to the women (and maybe men) who took the drug before me. I'm in a phase 1 trial, but before I joined the study a small number of people had already taken the drug, testing its safety. I'm not sure that I'd be brave enough to be first. It makes me feel a little less freaked out about being a test subject.

Being honest with myself can be really uncomfortable. Cancer is revealing my deepest, darkest hypocrisies while it shows me just how selfish I am. In my desperation to live, I find that I can, indeed, accept some collateral damage in the war under my skin.

Seeking

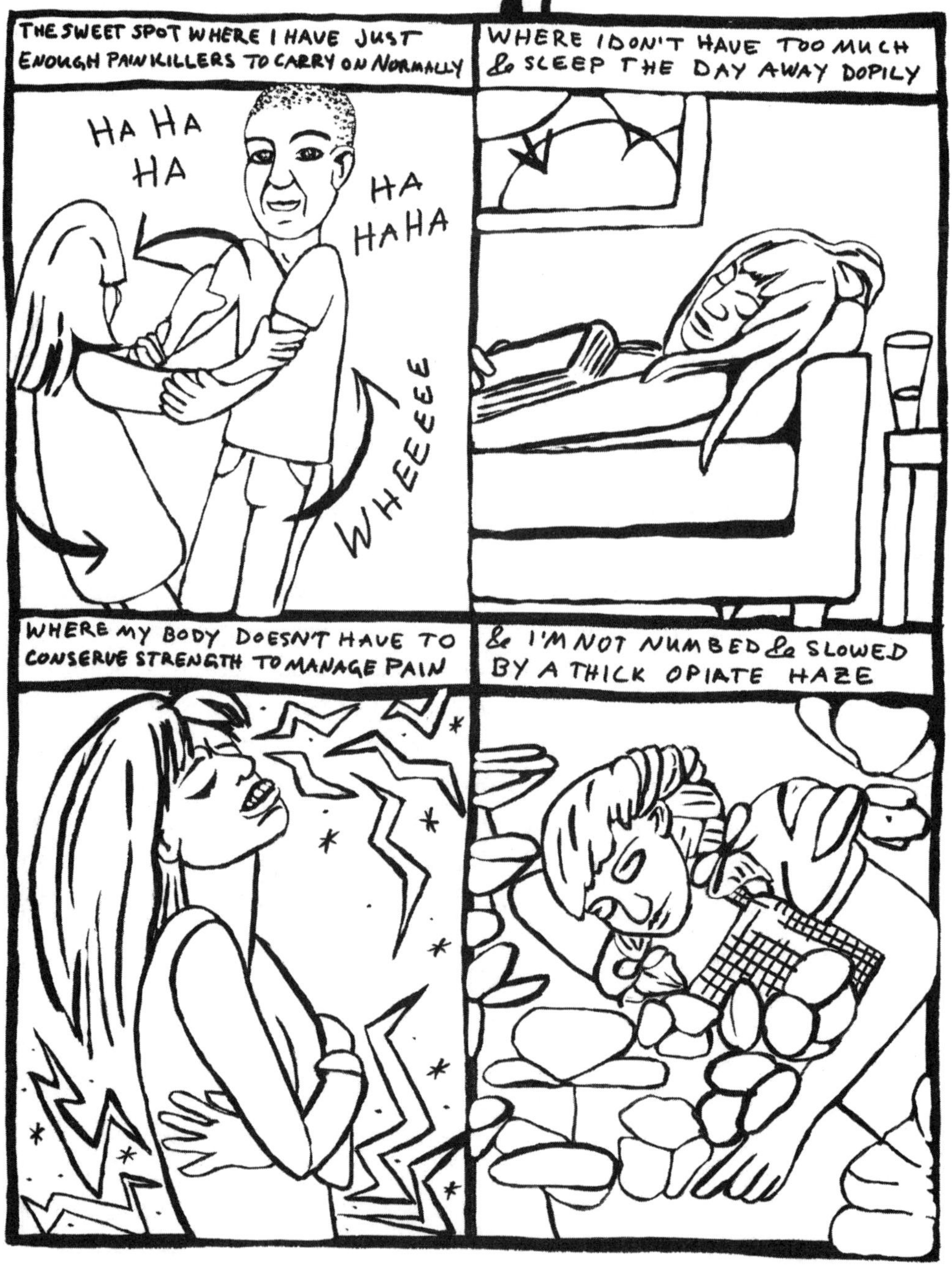
THE SWEET SPOT WHERE I HAVE JUST ENOUGH PAINKILLERS TO CARRY ON NORMALLY
HA HA HA
HA HAHA
WHEEEEEE
WHERE I DON'T HAVE TOO MUCH & SLEEP THE DAY AWAY DOPILY
WHERE MY BODY DOESN'T HAVE TO CONSERVE STRENGTH TO MANAGE PAIN
& I'M NOT NUMBED & SLOWED BY A THICK OPIATE HAZE

Seeking

I walk the thinnest line. So thin, it cuts into the balls of my feet.

If I stumble, if I step to either side, my day is ruined.

Too many painkillers, and I sleep the day away. It's really not so bad, except that I want so badly to fill my days with sweetness, to wring the most I can out of each of them.

And if I go out in the world without extra drugs, and the pain creeps in, it takes over. I am ruined.

Every day, I am seeking the sweet spot, the place where I can live my life more fully, forgetting, for a moment, that I am always living with cancer.

Side Effects

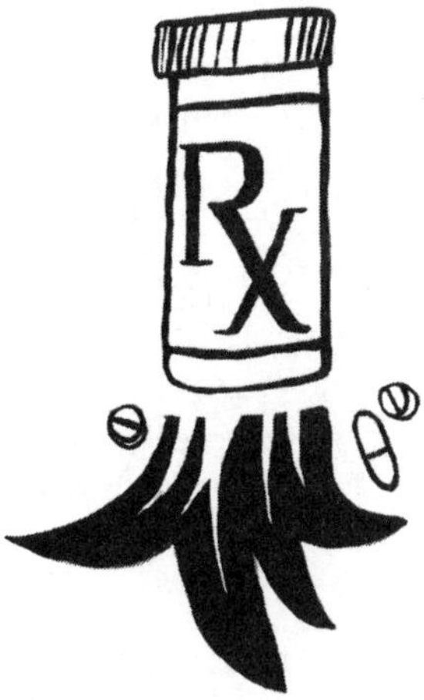
RX

WHAT CAN BE WITHSTOOD

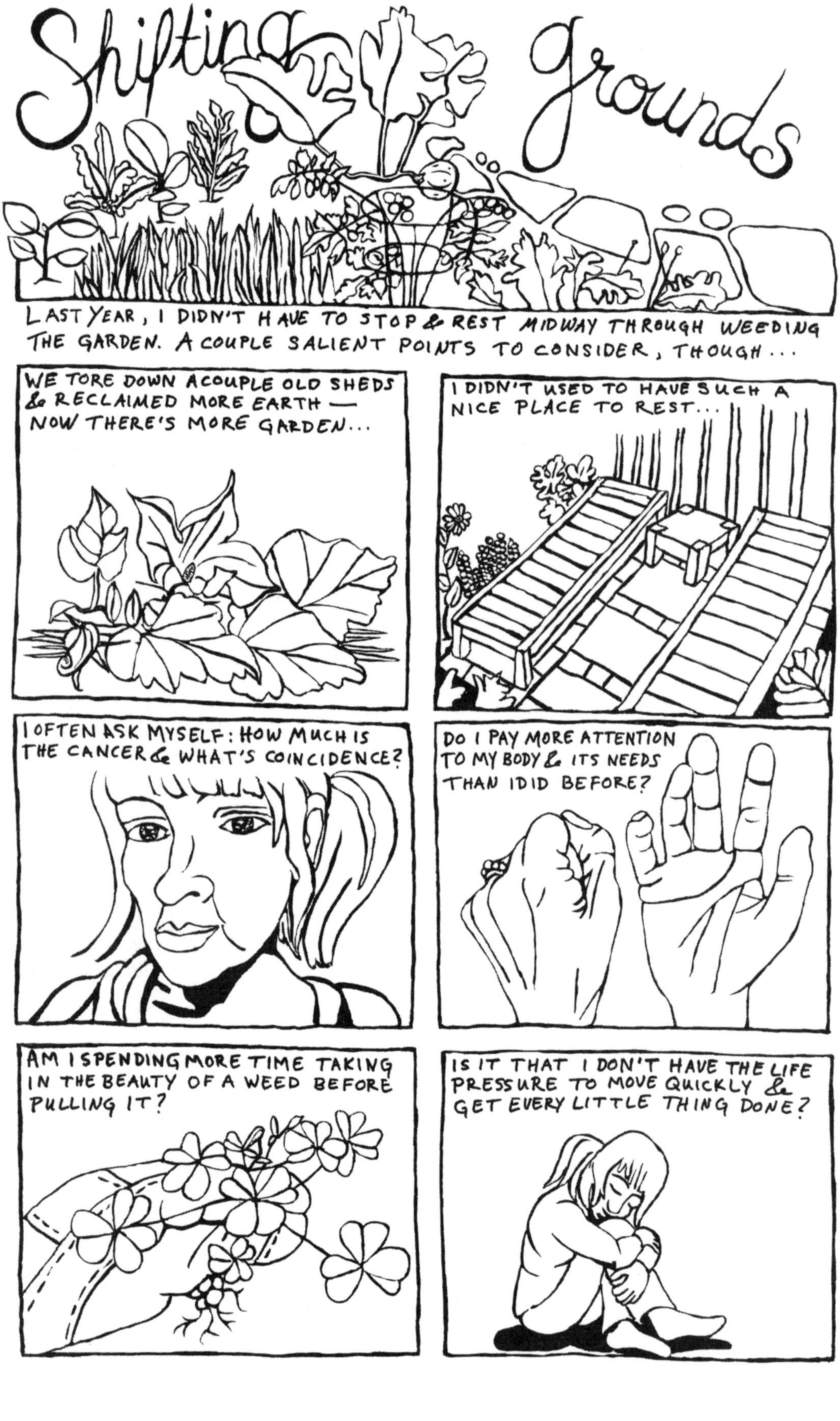
Shifting Grounds
LAST YEAR, I DIDN'T HAVE TO STOP & REST MIDWAY THROUGH WEEDING THE GARDEN. A COUPLE SALIENT POINTS TO CONSIDER, THOUGH...
WE TORE DOWN A COUPLE OLD SHEDS & RECLAIMED MORE EARTH — NOW THERE'S MORE GARDEN...
I DIDN'T USED TO HAVE SUCH A NICE PLACE TO REST...
I OFTEN ASK MYSELF: HOW MUCH IS THE CANCER & WHAT'S COINCIDENCE?
DO I PAY MORE ATTENTION TO MY BODY & ITS NEEDS THAN I DID BEFORE?
AM I SPENDING MORE TIME TAKING IN THE BEAUTY OF A WEED BEFORE PULLING IT?
IS IT THAT I DON'T HAVE THE LIFE PRESSURE TO MOVE QUICKLY & GET EVERY LITTLE THING DONE?

Shifting Grounds

I spend a lot of time thinking about myself. More than I ever have, or at least since I was a teenager.

Cancer thrusts you into the centre, while simultaneously pushing you outside. Friends stop themselves from sharing their problems, mumbling, "I mean, I have no right to bother you with my little problems. You have cancer." And in that moment, they've simultaneously raised me up and shut me out. It's a strange emotional tug of war.

Living with cancer means listening to my body. It means paying very close attention: resting when I'm tired, recording and reporting to my clinical trial nurse the most minute changes.

I have never been in such constant dialogue with my body.

Because I didn't pay as much attention before, it's difficult to know, really, where normal pain ends and cancer begins, when fatigue is caused by drugs, depression, or disease. The edges blur, while my awareness sharpens.

The Cancer Weight Loss Plan

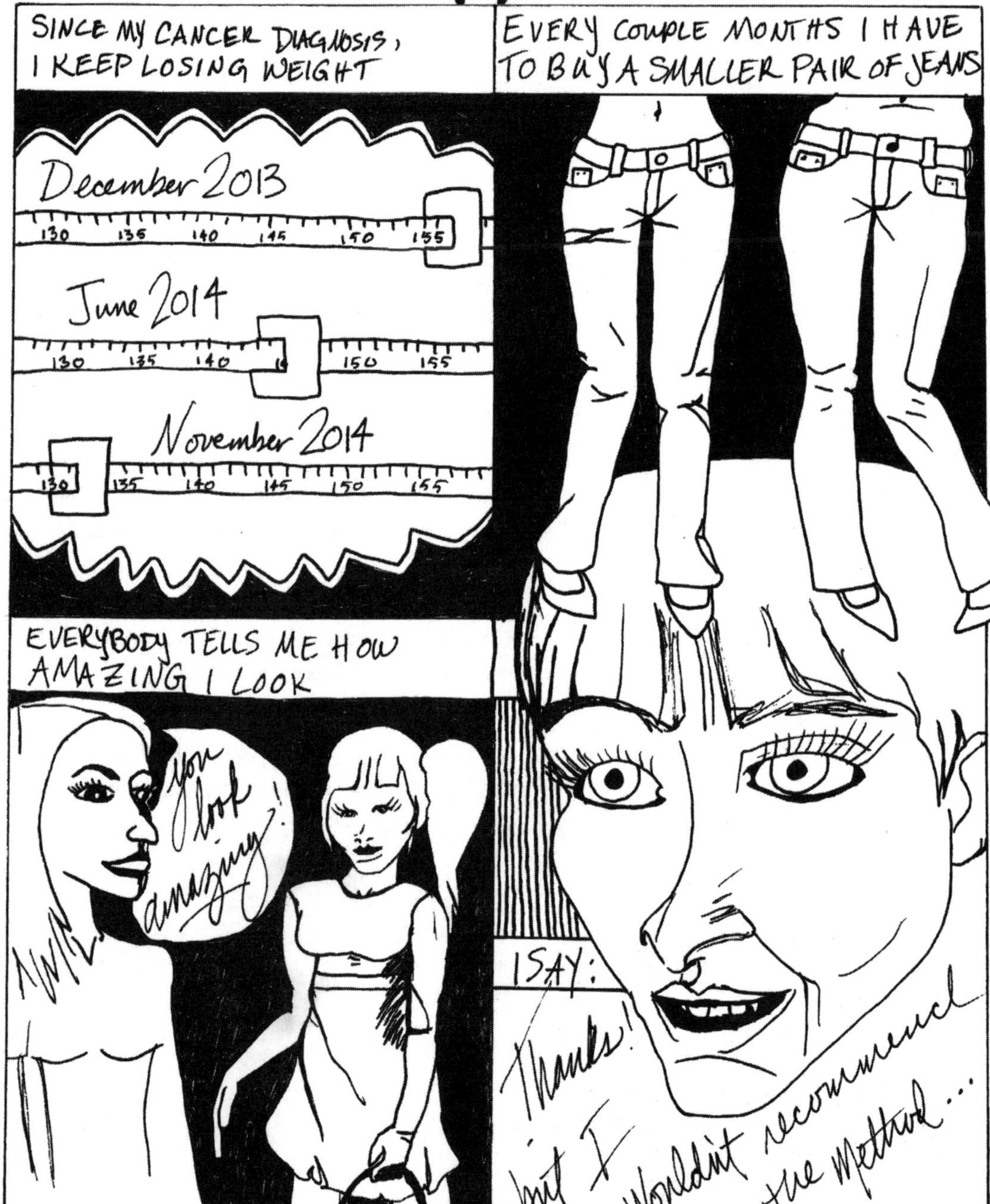

The Cancer Weight-Loss Plan

When I was first diagnosed, I cracked a joke to my nurse navigator, saying, "At least I'll lose some weight!"

Actually, she told me very seriously, chemo usually makes women "puffy." She seemed to get no delight from being a killjoy, but that didn't stop her from tarnishing my silver lining in the interest of honesty and good guidance.

Of course, that was before my bone scan. Before we knew that I was stage IV. When we were still looking for a cure. When we still thought I was going to start with chemo.

IN THE BEGINNING, every time they gave me a new drug, they would warn me that it might make me gain weight. What they weren't factoring in was my lifestyle changes. I have always been a vegetarian, and I have always eaten mostly whole foods, but when I got sick, I didn't want to put anything in my body that wasn't pure and healthy. The hormones in dairy freaked me out irrationally. I had no desire to get drunk. Sugar completely lost its appeal. I'd been putting up with gluten-induced eczema for years, but I suddenly couldn't stand it.

So I drew a line under it all, and even though I should have gained weight, I found myself steadily shrinking.

WITH CANCER, YOUR doctors don't worry as much about weight gain; they only worry about weight loss. They're afraid that you might have cachexia, that you might be wasting away to nothing.

So instead of celebrating as the pounds melted effortlessly away, I got nervous.

What if I keep losing weight? What if I disappear? Is that a better way out? Better than what? Is that how this naturally ends?

And then my first line of treatment failed and they gave me new meds, telling me: these might diminish your appetite.

So I choke down fat- and protein-rich smoothies in the morning like a body-builder. I eat whole avocados and snack on nuts. I try to keep eating as much as a normal person should, despite my diminished appetite. Which is a bit comical because I definitely used to eat much more than a normal person would.

And still, I shrink.

Cancer has so dramatically shaken up my body image that I'm not as fussed anymore about how I look in a bikini, whether I look chubby, sexy, lumpy, or strong. Although I wish I looked strong.

Don't get me wrong: my ego has not been eradicated. I still want to look good. I still wish I had the body I did at twenty. Doesn't nearly everybody?

But since diagnosis, what concerns me isn't how my body looks but what it can do. What does it mean to live in this body, healthy cells alongside rebellious ones? What can my body experience? And how can I make myself more comfortable?

Comfort means a lot of things. Being comfortable, as in living with as little pain as possible. Being comfortable with myself because really, why inflict harsh judgement over my shrinking size or diminishing abilities? Being comfortable with my own limitations and not pushing myself too hard. It means comfortable shoes and clothing I can wear all day at the hospital and that can be removed easily for scans and exams.

Putting my comfort first does not come naturally to me. I expect that can be said about most people, women especially. So it is a difficult shift for me, but an important one.

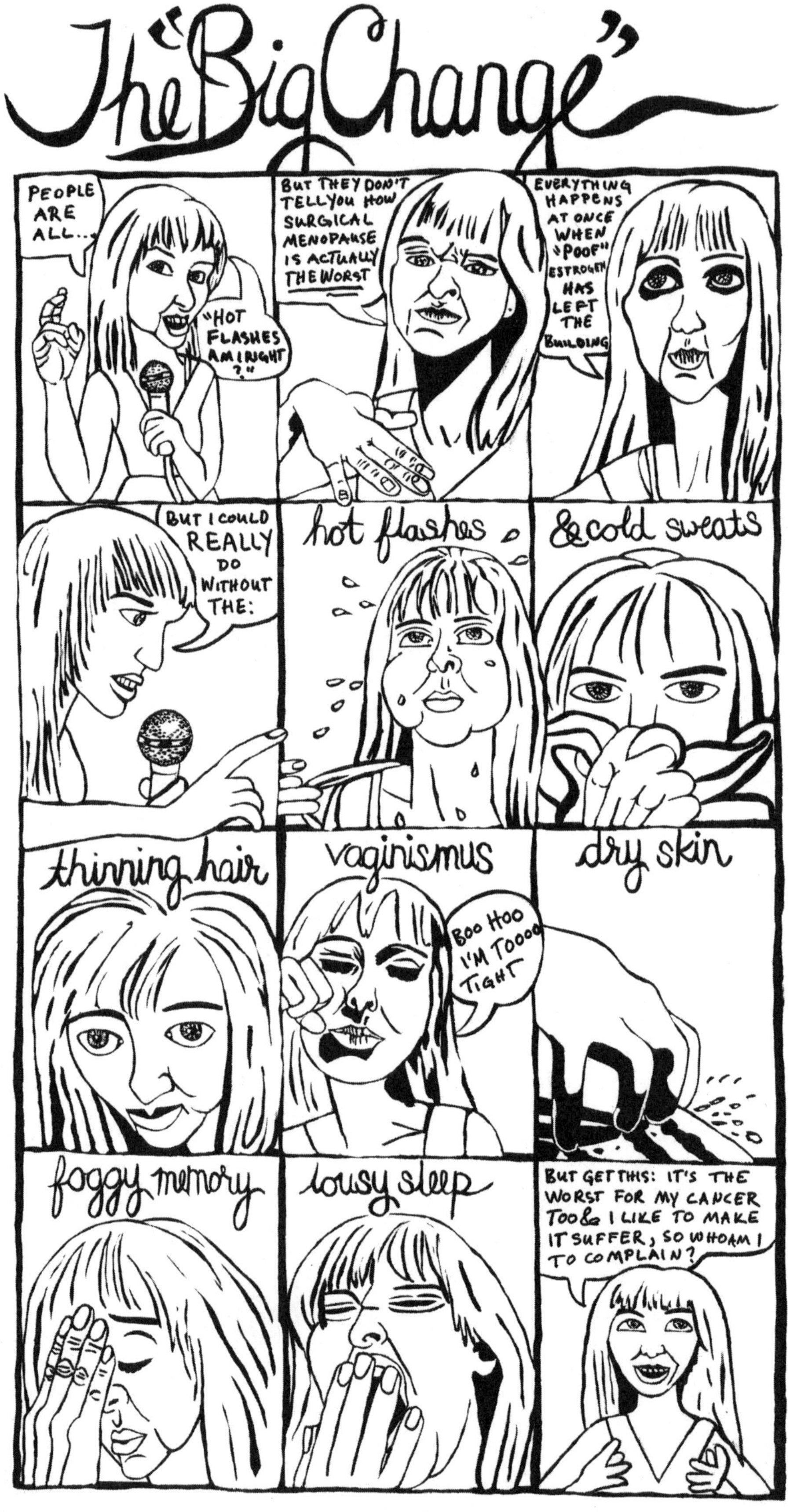
"The Big Change"
PEOPLE ARE ALL...
"HOT FLASHES AMIRIGHT?"
BUT THEY DON'T TELL YOU HOW SURGICAL MENOPAUSE IS ACTUALLY THE WORST
EVERYTHING HAPPENS AT ONCE WHEN "POOF" ESTROGEN HAS LEFT THE BUILDING
BUT I COULD REALLY DO WITHOUT THE:
hot flashes
& cold sweats
thinning hair
vaginismus
BOO HOO I'M TOOOO TIGHT
dry skin
foggy memory
lousy sleep
BUT GET THIS: IT'S THE WORST FOR MY CANCER TOO & I LIKE TO MAKE IT SUFFER, SO WHO AM I TO COMPLAIN?

The "Big Change"

Do we gloss over menopause because our society doesn't value the voice or experience of older women? Or do we clam up because sex makes us uncomfortable? Maybe especially elder sex?

We soften menopause by calling it the "big change," and then it is minimized. Reduced. No big deal.

Women awkwardly complain about temperature, as if it's nothing for the body to flush into full wet, sweat making our clothes heavy and hair limp. And although we do hear about hot flashes, we don't usually talk about the cold sweats that follow them like a kid sister.

Sometimes you hear women talking about how much less important sex is for them, or how much more.

Many women have told me it's not that bad.

But that's really where the conversation ends.

WE DON'T REALLY talk about what happens to younger women who have abrupt menopause because of a surgery (elective or not) or chemo.

I'll grant that not every woman's experience is the same. Not every person gets every possible side effect or symptom (except those who do). And we do not yet have a way of telling what will affect who, and how.

Still, we need to talk. We need to talk about young women and what might happen in their menopause.

Because this is what happened to me: in my twisted little mind, I thought I'd done something wrong, that I must not have followed my doctor's instructions

because menopause hit me all at once. And then it got worse.

With every other treatment, my doctors and I had long conversations about what I might experience. These discussions covered clear and easy-to-understand potential side effects.

Not so when my oncologist recommended a bilateral salpingo-oophorectomy. (It's a true mouthful, and I feel like a champ when I spell it correctly.) Here's what it means: it's an out-patient laparoscopic surgery in which they remove the ovaries and the fallopian tubes. Because, get this, even if the ovaries are gone, ovarian cancer can occur in the fallopian tubes, which are completely useless without the ovaries.

My oncologist and my OB/GYN surgeon told me that I might experience some menopausal symptoms, such as hot flashes and night sweats, maybe some vaginal dryness. They made it sound like no big deal. And really, it's nothing if it helps me to live longer. But my menopause is not no big deal.

Maybe they didn't want to scare me with all sorts of potential symptoms that might not apply to me, but I see it another way: Tell me the worst that can happen, and then I can feel lucky if I don't experience it, yet prepared if I do. Is that really such a terrible thing?

Because when the hot flashes got bad, I had to plan for them with complicated layer changes, no matter the weather. As the estrogen disappeared from my body, all the luscious curves melted off my frame, and I spent lots of money buying new bras to make up for the changes but still provide support so my back wasn't killing me.

But the worst of it is the vaginismus. No longer employed in the possibility of procreation, my vagina just dried up and closed up shop.

The soft words used to describe menopause don't prepare you when your menopause isn't gradual but sudden and complete.

So how do we talk about menopause?

Because it's different for every woman. How do we prepare each other, so we aren't left in the dark, blaming ourselves?

It's not just that we need to talk more — we talk a lot — but we have to talk about the right things.

And we have to listen to the women who went through it before us. I know that somewhere — if I could have just found her — there was a woman who could have told me that I was not alone.

And that would have changed everything.

Splitting Hairs

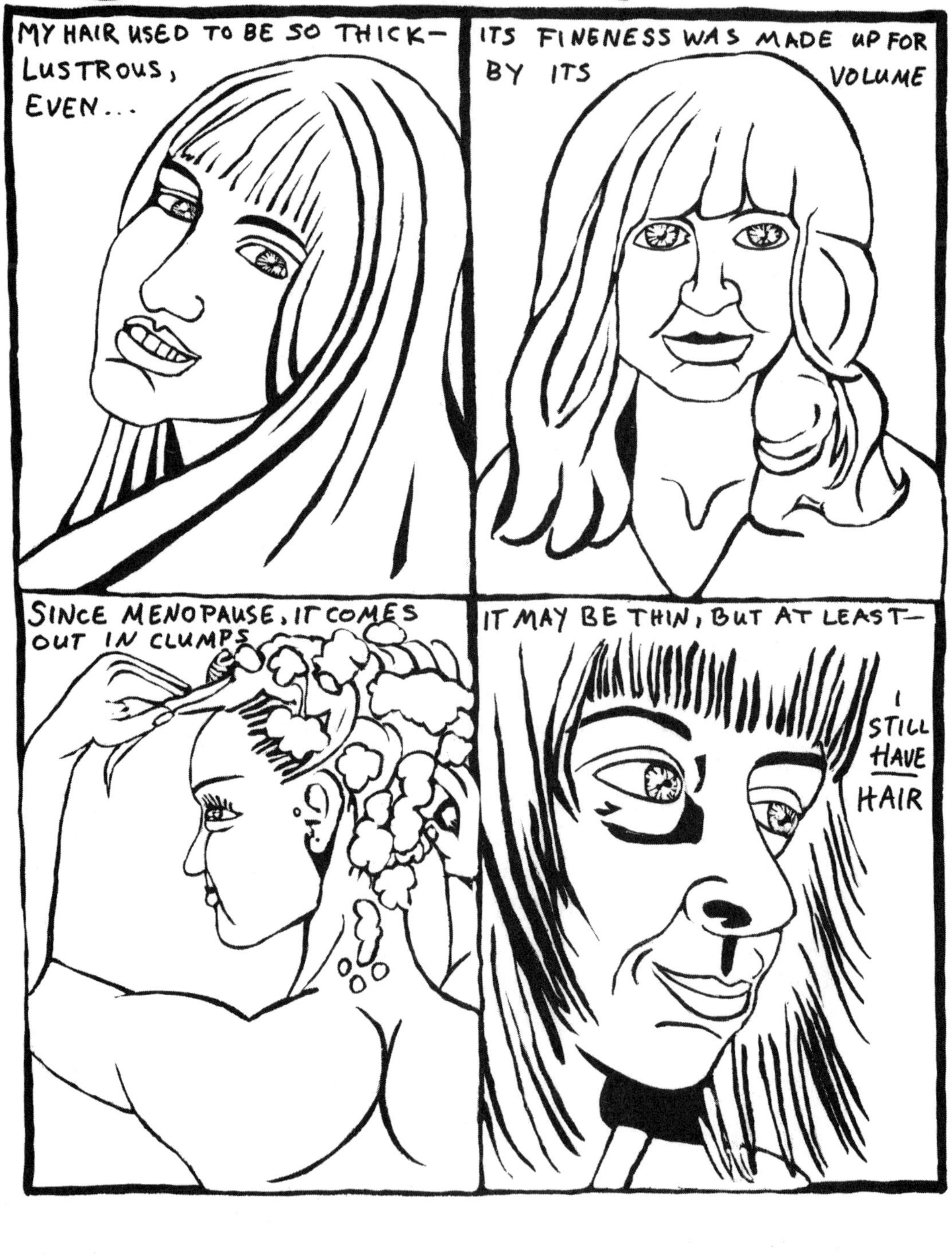
MY HAIR USED TO BE SO THICK—
LUSTROUS,
EVEN...
ITS FINENESS WAS MADE UP FOR
BY ITS VOLUME
SINCE MENOPAUSE, IT COMES OUT IN CLUMPS
IT MAY BE THIN, BUT AT LEAST—
I STILL HAVE HAIR

Splitting Hairs

When I was little, my big sister told me to grow my hair out, not perm it, and I'd thank her for her advice later. I took her words to heart and grew my hair long. By high school, it tumbled, lustrous, thick, all the way down my back. It had an identity of its own, reaching out its tentacles to pull people closer. It caught in car doors and had to be moved when I used the toilet.

A couple years into university, I bleached it a blinding sheet of platinum blonde and started to cut away at it. Piece by piece, I cut it shorter, trying out every hairstyle I'd never had. Eventually, my hair was so short that I could cut it by feeling its length with the width of my fingers. I suppose I'm lucky, in a way, that I had so much to lose.

Since menopause began, my hair comes out in handfuls in the shower. It's a wonder that I still have enough hair to style, that I don't look like a cancer patient.

homework

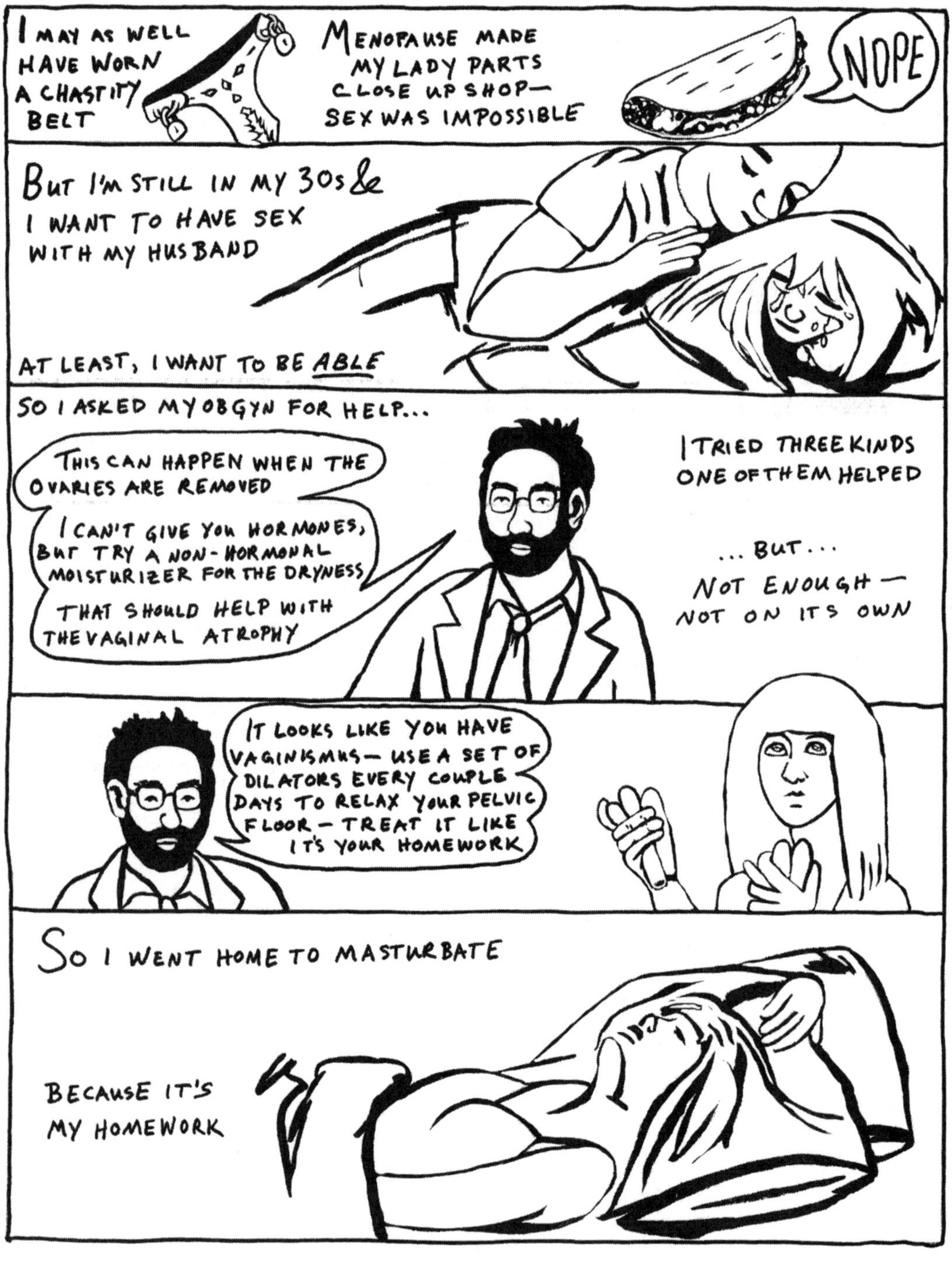

I MAY AS WELL HAVE WORN A CHASTITY BELT
MENOPAUSE MADE MY LADY PARTS CLOSE UP SHOP— SEX WAS IMPOSSIBLE
NOPE
BUT I'M STILL IN MY 30s & I WANT TO HAVE SEX WITH MY HUSBAND
AT LEAST, I WANT TO BE ABLE
SO I ASKED MY OBGYN FOR HELP...
THIS CAN HAPPEN WHEN THE OVARIES ARE REMOVED
I CAN'T GIVE YOU HORMONES, BUT TRY A NON-HORMONAL MOISTURIZER FOR THE DRYNESS
THAT SHOULD HELP WITH THE VAGINAL ATROPHY
I TRIED THREE KINDS ONE OF THEM HELPED
...BUT...
NOT ENOUGH— NOT ON ITS OWN
IT LOOKS LIKE YOU HAVE VAGINISMUS— USE A SET OF DILATORS EVERY COUPLE DAYS TO RELAX YOUR PELVIC FLOOR— TREAT IT LIKE IT'S YOUR HOMEWORK
SO I WENT HOME TO MASTURBATE
BECAUSE IT'S MY HOMEWORK

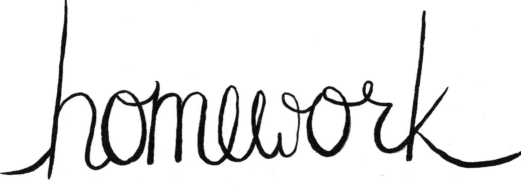

Homework

Vaginismus sounds like a medieval torture device that belongs in a stone tower. I've been struggling with it since my oophorectomy, when my vagina realized that it was never going to need to allow a baby through and retired early. Without the biological imperative, the body took away the resources that were being used to keep my lady parts running smoothly.

Nobody had warned me about the possibility of vaginismus, so I completely freaked out. Sex was more than painful—it was downright impossible. A few tear-filled nights and my sweet husband was afraid to touch me, afraid to hurt me.

But I was still in my thirties, with a husband I loved very much, and I wanted the option of a sex life.

I had a lot of uncomfortable conversations with men about my body and my sex life.

I said the same things over and over.

My oncologist suggested that I talk to my palliative team. They referred me to a nurse who called me once while I was walking through an airport, and then never returned my calls. I googled "menopause" and learned that vaginismus is common, not just with young women. I talked to my OB/GYN surgeon. He recommended a vaginal moisturizer. It was strange and unhelpful. It kind of stung. I couldn't have hormones because of my cancer, so I worked my way through the very short list of three non-hormonal vaginal moisturizers available in Canada. I was so grateful when the third one helped a bit. For it to keep working, I had to use it every few days. Forever.

Yet even though the moisturizer helped, it was not enough to allow me to have pain-free sex, so I went back to my OB/GYN. He told me to move on to a set of dilators, which were basically medical-grade dildos, gradually increasing in size. He told me I might want a vibrator to help me relax with the dilator. I told him that I already had one and he smiled kindly. "Good." He said that I needed to relax. My anxiety about not being able to have sex was making it worse. My anxiety was causing every muscle to clench, including those in the pelvic floor, which needed to be relaxed to allow penetration.

This man was so kind and patient. He had the softest man-hands I'd ever shaken. He listened and told me not to worry, this was common and treatable, I could get through this.

I asked him if it would require maintenance.

Yes, he told me. If I was not having sex every couple of days, I would need to use the dilators for at least fifteen minutes instead.

"Were you good at doing your homework?" he asked me. I nodded. "You'll be fine."

So this will always be my life now, depending on what I want my life to be. Until, maybe, it isn't. Because menopause passes, if I can just live long enough.

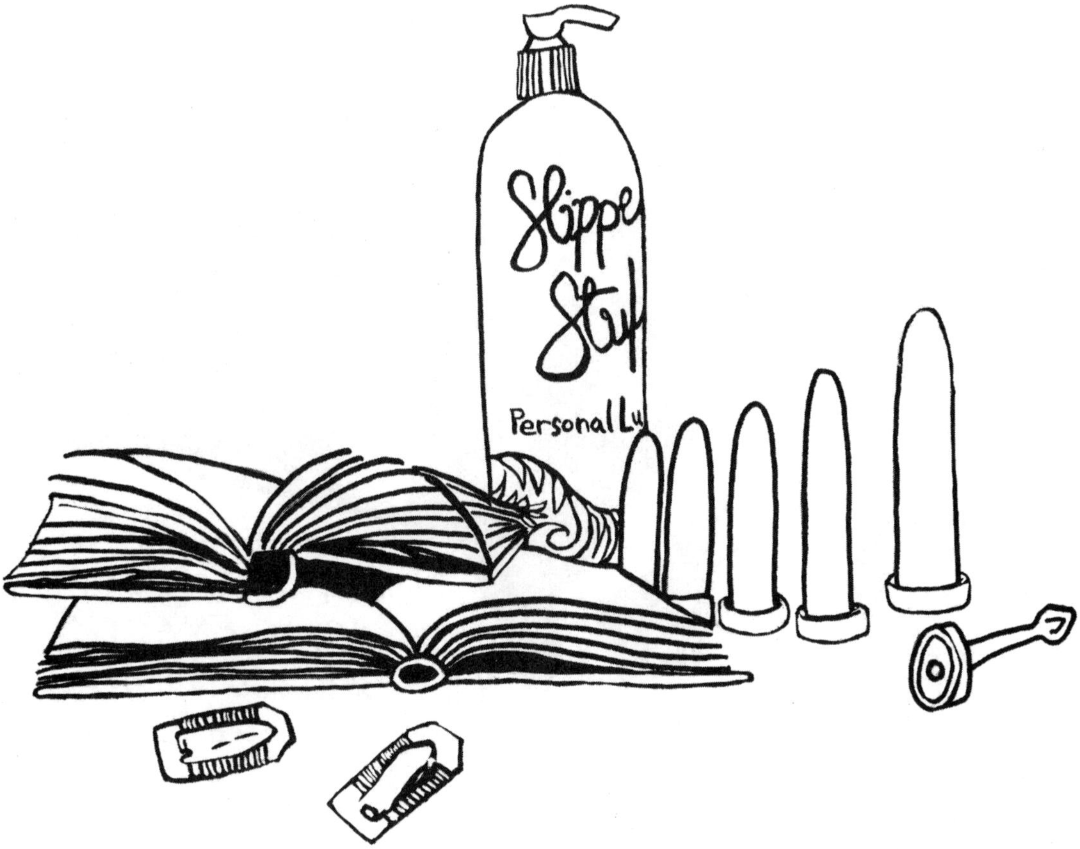
Personal Lu

Do You Like That?

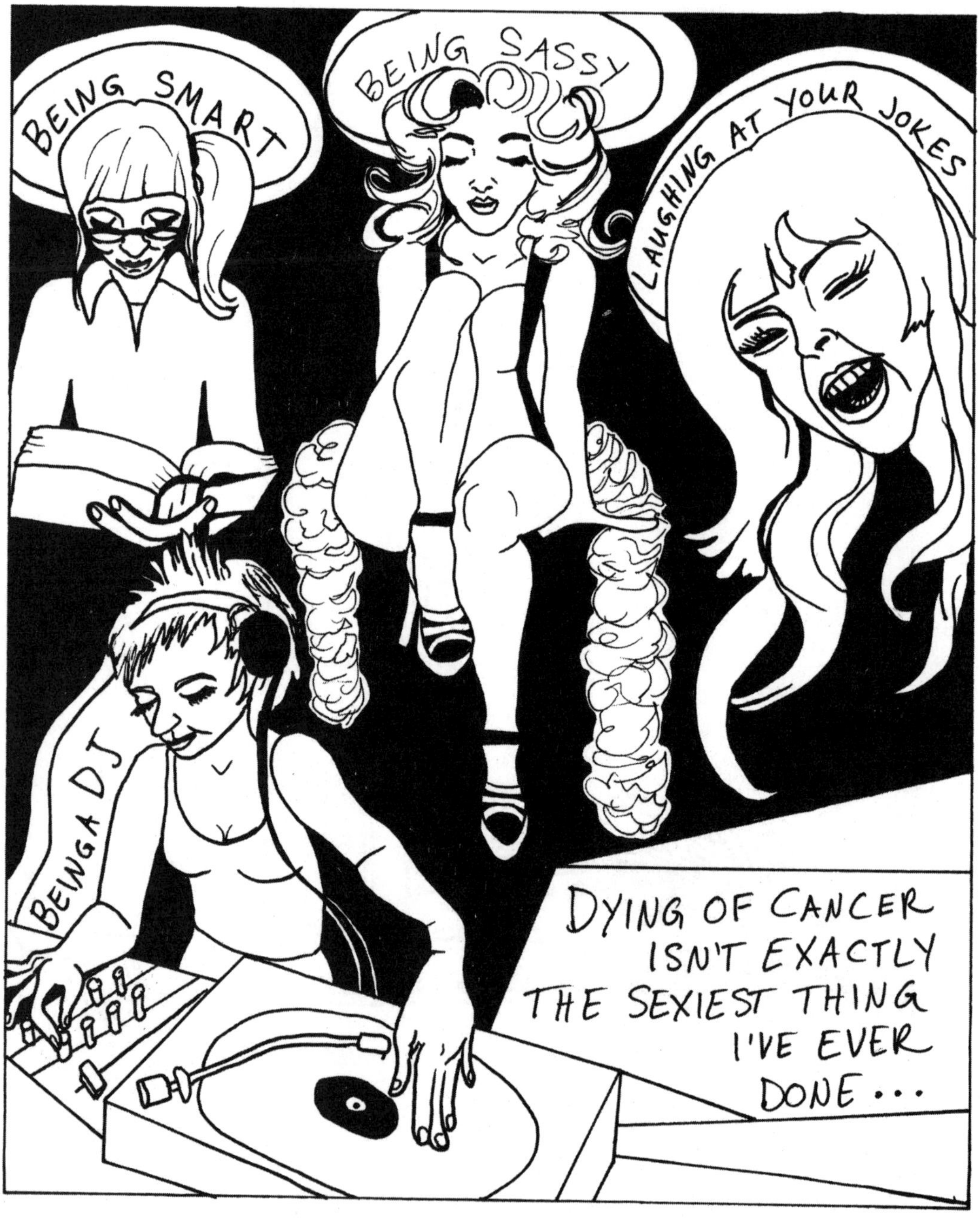
BEING SMART
BEING SASSY
LAUGHING AT YOUR JOKES
BEING A DJ
DYING OF CANCER ISN'T EXACTLY THE SEXIEST THING I'VE EVER DONE...

Do You Like That?

Riddle me this: If sex is the stuff of life, and cancer is incremental death, what am I?

Because it's not about how I look (which is pretty awesome). It's not as simple as how I feel in any given moment (generally, less awesome). Complications are deep, twisted, malformed. Side effects from treatment: sexual dysfunction, diminished self-worth, a sense that my body is betraying me.

And it's the viscera, the stuff of excrement and bile, the dirty side of living, writ large.

Pretty. Bubbly. Sparkly. Um...cancery? One of these things just doesn't belong.

So we put some spin on incurable and call it chronic. As science advances, more women will die *with* instead of *from* this disease: they will carry a stable, or *managed*, cancer to an unrelated end.

I hope and plan to be one of these women, but that still means that I will be living in cancer's shadow for the rest of my life.

Can't Be Trusted

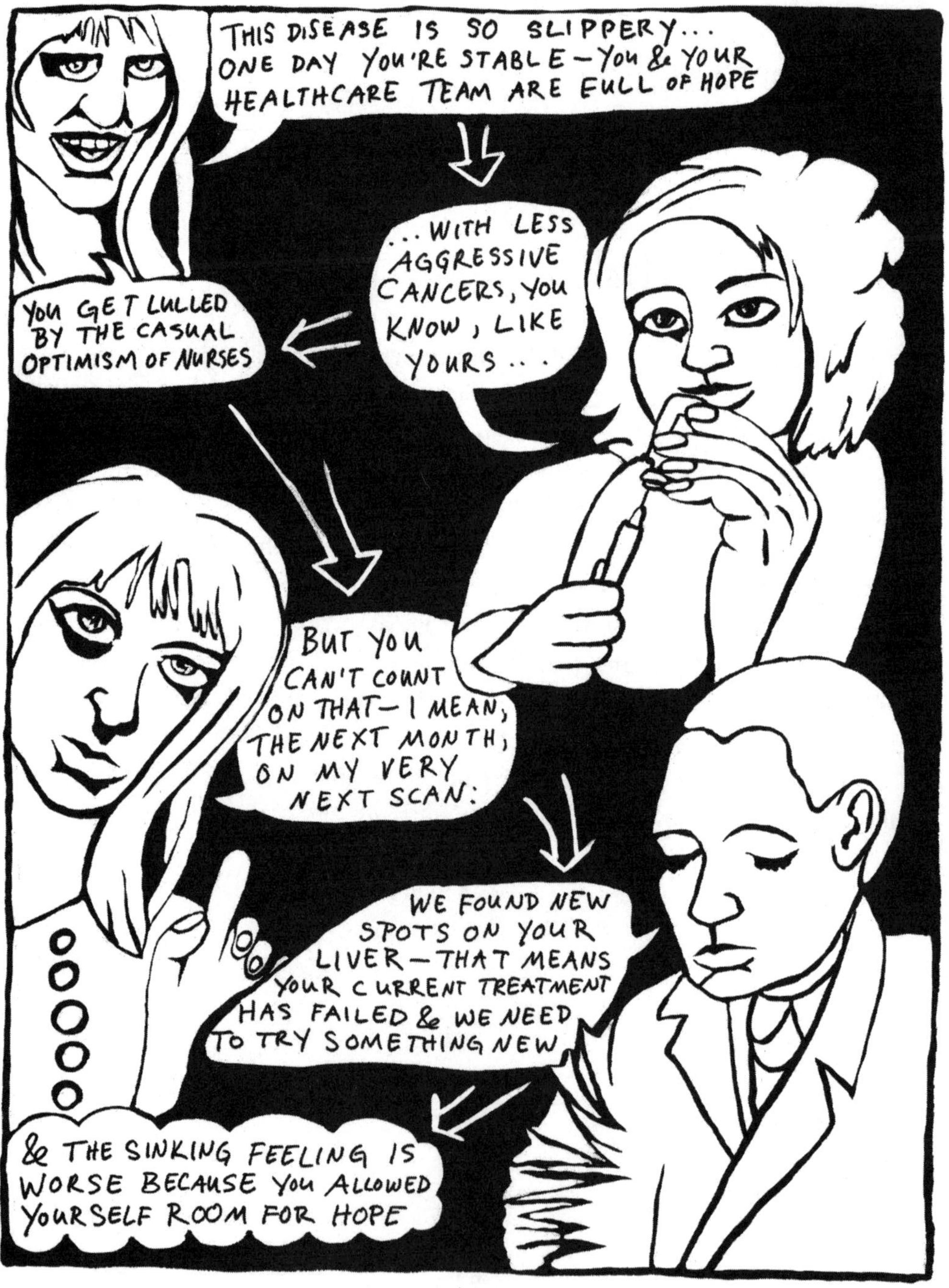
THIS DISEASE IS SO SLIPPERY... ONE DAY YOU'RE STABLE—YOU & YOUR HEALTHCARE TEAM ARE FULL OF HOPE
...WITH LESS AGGRESSIVE CANCERS, YOU KNOW, LIKE YOURS...
YOU GET LULLED BY THE CASUAL OPTIMISM OF NURSES
BUT YOU CAN'T COUNT ON THAT—I MEAN, THE NEXT MONTH, ON MY VERY NEXT SCAN:
WE FOUND NEW SPOTS ON YOUR LIVER—THAT MEANS YOUR CURRENT TREATMENT HAS FAILED & WE NEED TO TRY SOMETHING NEW
& THE SINKING FEELING IS WORSE BECAUSE YOU ALLOWED YOURSELF ROOM FOR HOPE

Can't Be Trusted

Hope is a dangerous thing. It's absolutely crucial all the time, or I couldn't go on. I am a naturally optimistic person, and I am inclined to hope for the moon. But I can't put too much hope in any one thing.

Especially now. In one moment, everything can change.

The reality of advanced cancer is that if we manage to stabilize it, it's only stable for an indeterminate while. My disease is highly adaptive, constantly trying to figure out how to get around whatever obstacle my doctors and I put in front of it. And it's only ever a matter of time before it finds a way around the barricades and begins to grow again or set up shop somewhere new.

And when it does, we change the treatment, hoping to stall it in its tracks again. The order of treatments is like this: first, the most easily tolerated drugs; then each subsequent treatment comes with new, more difficult side effects.

In the beginning, in addition to the primary tumour in my left breast, I had metastases in three bones and two lymph nodes.

My first line of treatment lasted about eleven months. By ten months, I was starting to feel that I was going to be okay. I started to dream bigger, to think about going back to work, to hope that I might be one of those lucky women who manages to live a long time with this disease, that I might even live long enough for scientists to find out how to stop my cancer in a more meaningful way.

While giving me my bone-strengthening injection, a nurse even described my cancer as "less aggressive." I was over the moon. Which made the fall much worse when I found out the next month that my cancer had spread to a shiny new organ: my liver.

That's why I need to be careful. Hope is delicious, heady stuff, but reality has a way of upsetting the applecart.

I have to find a way to balance the hope I need to get up every day with the pragmatism I need to deal with bad news.

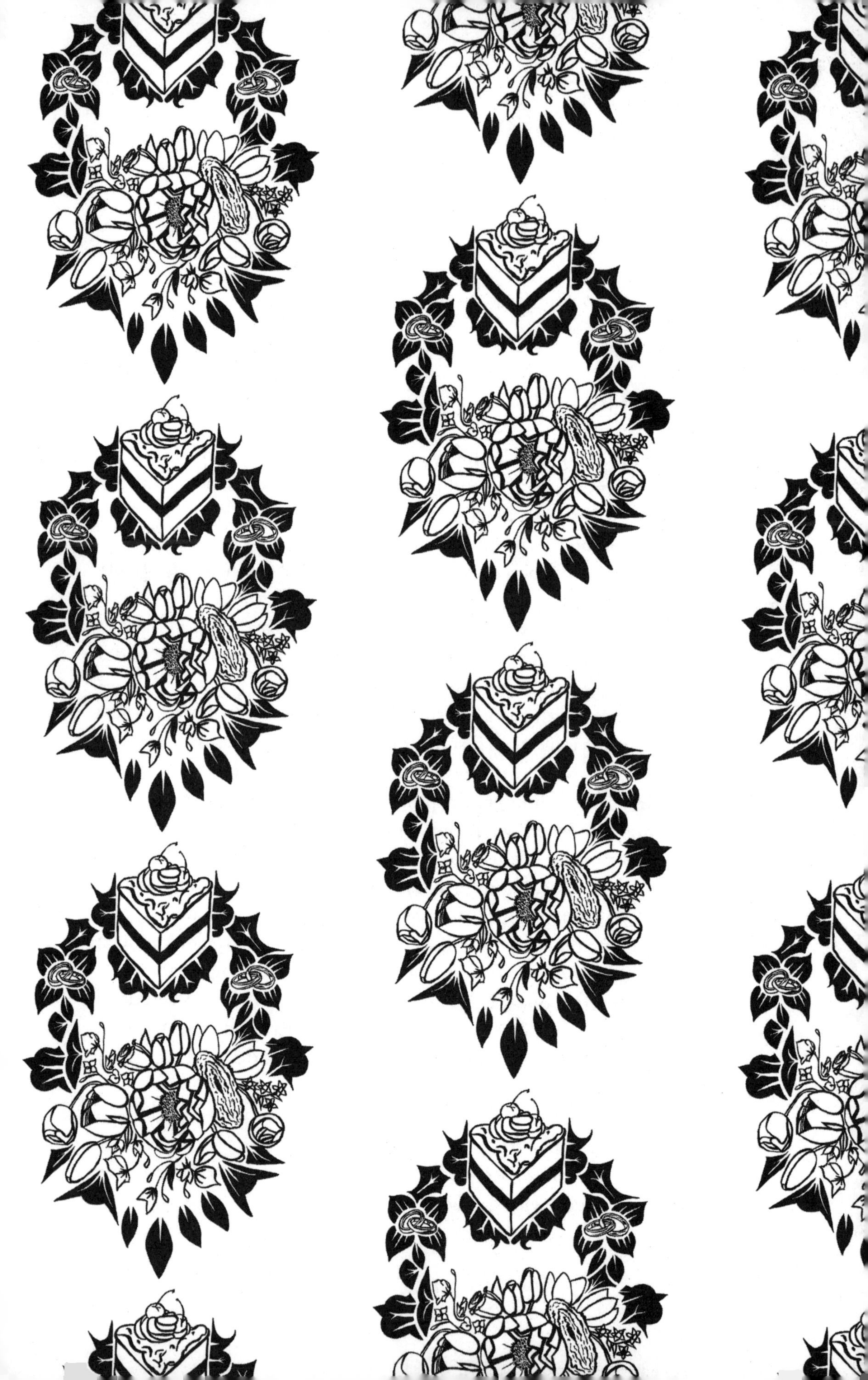

PART TWO

Marriage

LOVE CHANGES EVERYTHING

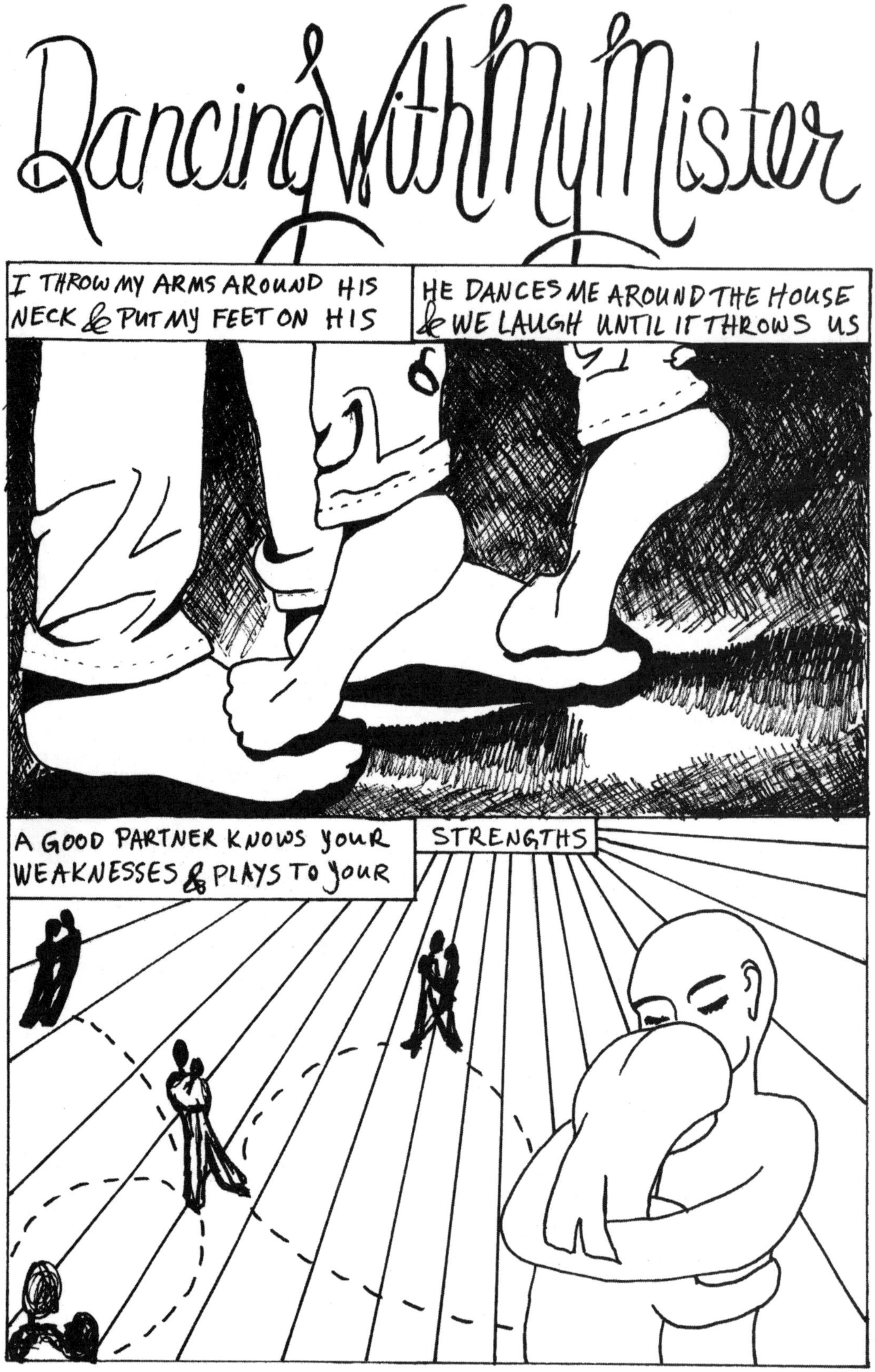

Dancing With My Mister
I THROW MY ARMS AROUND HIS NECK & PUT MY FEET ON HIS
HE DANCES ME AROUND THE HOUSE & WE LAUGH UNTIL IT THROWS US
A GOOD PARTNER KNOWS YOUR WEAKNESSES & PLAYS TO YOUR
STRENGTHS

Dancing with My Mister

Since I moved to Canada to marry him, David and I have rarely been apart for more than a few days at a time. We love each other's company.

Since I got sick, it's been harder for us to be apart. He travels for work often, but not for long. And when I travel alone, it's usually to visit my family. When we're together, we hold one another so closely.

And if I let myself slip into the edge of the vast quicksand of melancholy, he can usually spin me back, dancing me closer to this life and all its remarkable treasures, of which he is my most precious and dear.

And when he pulls me close, nudging his feet under mine, twirling me around the house, I feel loved. And I feel hope that this moment will repeat again and again for years to come.

Once Upon A Time

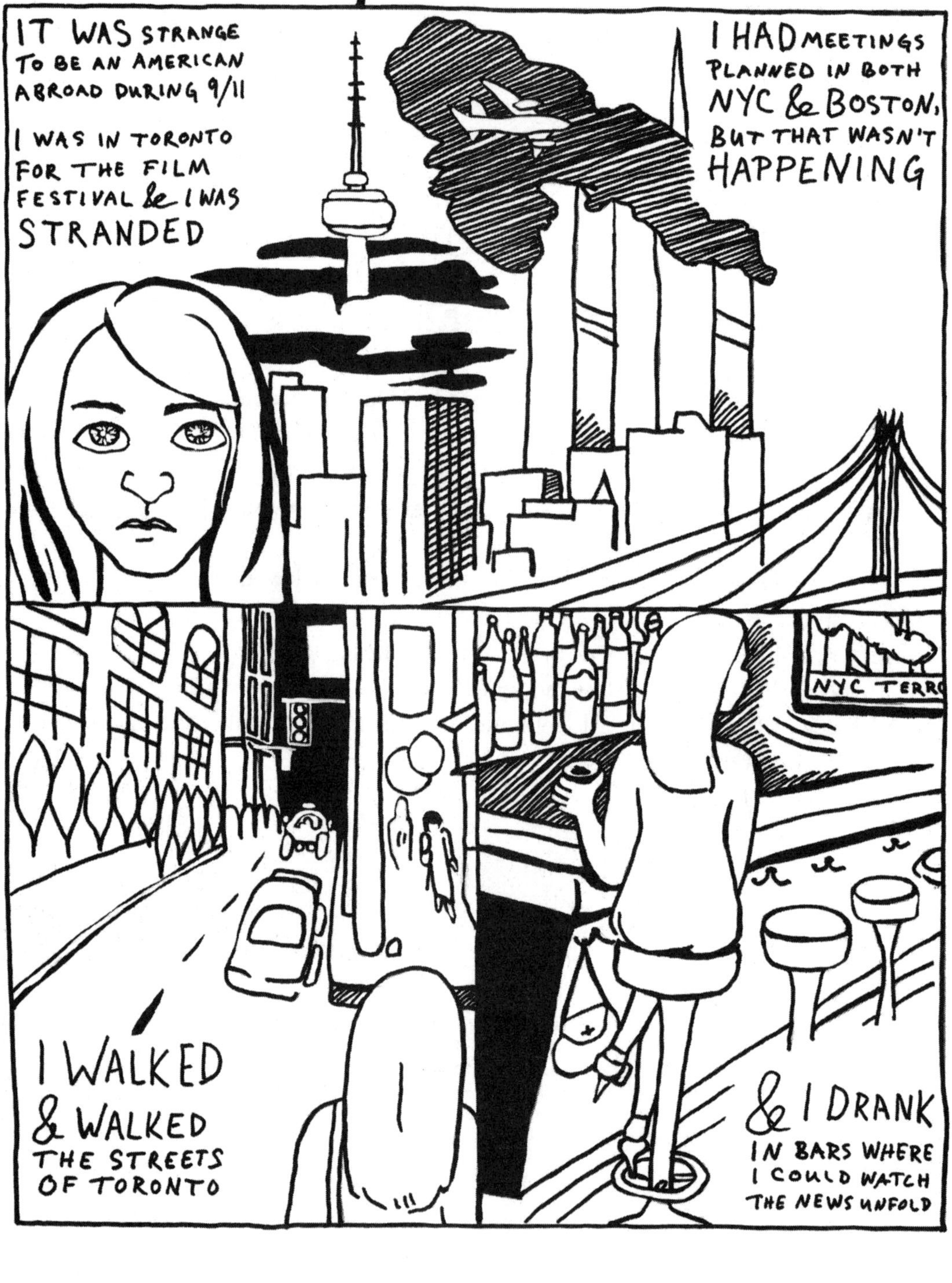

IT WAS STRANGE TO BE AN AMERICAN ABROAD DURING 9/11
I WAS IN TORONTO FOR THE FILM FESTIVAL & I WAS STRANDED
I HAD MEETINGS PLANNED IN BOTH NYC & BOSTON, BUT THAT WASN'T HAPPENING
NYC TERRO
I WALKED & WALKED THE STREETS OF TORONTO
& I DRANK IN BARS WHERE I COULD WATCH THE NEWS UNFOLD

The World Was Burning

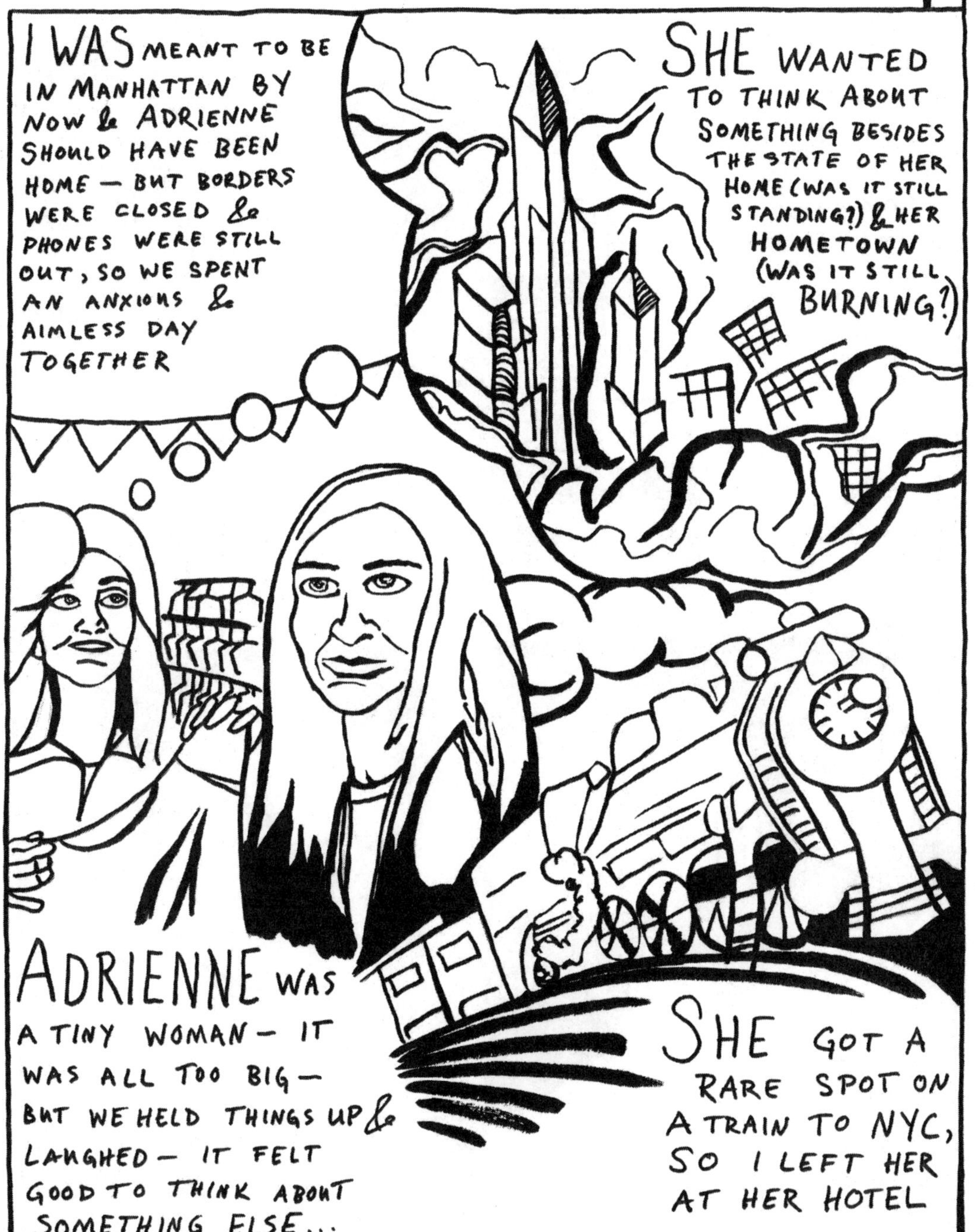
I WAS MEANT TO BE IN MANHATTAN BY NOW & ADRIENNE SHOULD HAVE BEEN HOME — BUT BORDERS WERE CLOSED & PHONES WERE STILL OUT, SO WE SPENT AN ANXIOUS & AIMLESS DAY TOGETHER
SHE WANTED TO THINK ABOUT SOMETHING BESIDES THE STATE OF HER HOME (WAS IT STILL STANDING?) & HER HOMETOWN (WAS IT STILL BURNING?)
ADRIENNE WAS A TINY WOMAN — IT WAS ALL TOO BIG — BUT WE HELD THINGS UP & LAUGHED — IT FELT GOOD TO THINK ABOUT SOMETHING ELSE...
SHE GOT A RARE SPOT ON A TRAIN TO NYC, SO I LEFT HER AT HER HOTEL

I Was Falling In Love

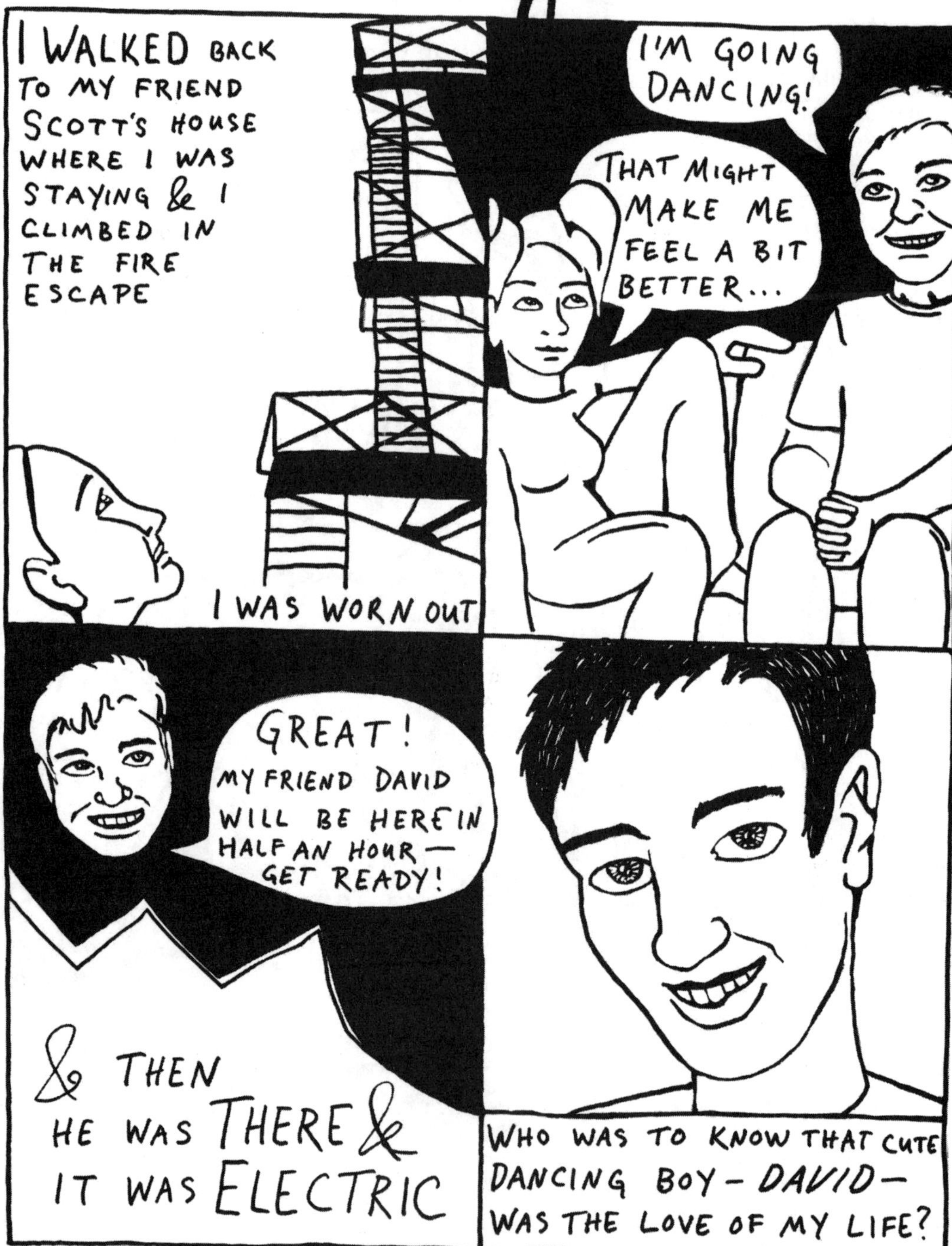

I WALKED BACK TO MY FRIEND SCOTT'S HOUSE WHERE I WAS STAYING & I CLIMBED IN THE FIRE ESCAPE
I WAS WORN OUT
I'M GOING DANCING!
THAT MIGHT MAKE ME FEEL A BIT BETTER...
GREAT! MY FRIEND DAVID WILL BE HERE IN HALF AN HOUR — GET READY!
& THEN HE WAS THERE & IT WAS ELECTRIC
WHO WAS TO KNOW THAT CUTE DANCING BOY — DAVID — WAS THE LOVE OF MY LIFE?

Once Upon A Time / The World Was Burning / I Was Falling In Love

He was such a pretty boy. Slight and strong, with eyelashes for miles and straight brown hair that made his blue eyes pop. At the centre of each eye, a hazel sunflower seemed to bloom just for me.

He warned me that night that he talked a lot, then said almost nothing as we danced for hours on the cantilevered floor of the Palais Royale. All the jumping and stomping at the rave made my water bottle skitter away across the floor, and he chased after it, through the flying feet of a mess of sweaty dancers. When he handed it back to me, he pulled me close, pressing his lips against mine. My legs went out beneath me. Then, as quickly as he'd taken hold of me, he let me go with a bashful smile.

Later, in the taxi, he put his head on my shoulder and asked if he could come home with me. Home was the sofa bed in Scott's living room, but that didn't stop us.

We kissed and traced the edges of each other's bodies until dawn. We kept our clothes mostly on, not ready to let go of the mystery, to give in to the intensity of our desire.

In some ways, we were still trying to be good. We both lived with other people. I'm not just making retroactive excuses when I say that both relationships were already in steady decline. We were both coasting in poor matches because breaking up is hard and we were generally conflict averse. Yet we tried to tell ourselves that we were respecting our bad matches by not actually having sex.

It was no use. We'd already fallen in love.

I CALLED THE airline and they were only too happy to change my flight, letting me stay in Toronto another week. Nobody wanted to fly.

Monday I walked the streets, making up love songs and singing them to myself. I stopped at a payphone and left myself a chirpy message so I wouldn't forget how this felt. I barely touched the ground.

Tuesday, David could get away for a date. We had a reservation at a restaurant, but when I climbed into the car and kissed him, that plan was abandoned.

We careened toward a hole in the wall called Squirly's. The only open table was in the centre of the room under a bright lamp. We drank bourbon, ate hungrily, and looked at each other like wolves. We were probably a spectacle, and we thought our server was a bit uncomfortable, so we tipped especially well.

He was a flame and I was a moth.

Half an hour later we were in a dark park. We stumbled toward the dark end of the athletic field, tearing at each other's clothes.

As we tumbled across the soft grass, he whispered "*Je t'aime.*" Maybe he felt safer professing his love so soon in French rather than English. He was so quiet that I had to ask him to repeat himself. "*Je t'aime!*" he said. My heart pounding to bursting, I pulled him closer and said, "I love you, too."

He was mine and I was unequivocally his.

Already.

WHEN I WENT back to Seattle at the end of the week, I found a new place to live. Even if my perfect week in Toronto with David was all I ever got with him, it had opened my eyes. No matter what happened with that perfect sweet boy, I couldn't go back to being miserable in my decrepit relationship. And this way, by the time I saw him again, I would be free to see where our connection went.

The next few months were a frenzy of cross-country flights. A weekend here, a week there, and in order to see him for New Year's Eve, I had to go to his parents' house for the holidays. They were very welcoming and kind. I arrived the day after Christmas, a Jew with a suitcase full of Christmas presents.

They put us in the basement, far from the other bedrooms. There wasn't the faintest sly wink, but they knew what they were doing: protecting their own innocence.

Five months after we met, I visited for Valentine's Day. David knew it had never been my favourite holiday and had the good sense to wait until the fifteenth to propose. We danced all night again, and in the cold, clear light of dawn, he got down on one knee in our tiny hotel room and asked me to marry him. Speechless with shock and love, I didn't answer right away, so he asked again. When I managed, breathless, to say yes, we fell down onto the clean white sheets and cried with joy and relief.

I had no idea that, since he met me, he'd been sleeping on a friend's couch to save up for a ring. He was so sure from the very first. Even though we'd only been in each other's presence for a few weeks, we spoke for hours every day. We wrote long letters. We made mix tapes, and I sent him flowers and chocolates while he sent me books. He promised to keep me in books for the rest of my life. In fact, he still curates a pre-vetted to-read shelf for me of books he thinks I'll enjoy.

Two months after he proposed, we decided to elope. I was visiting and we couldn't find a single reason to wait, so I found a justice of the peace who would marry us out of his home office on the lake. One long-lapsed Catholic and one secular Jew, we asked for his shortest ceremony, no god. We bought beautiful clothes that we could wear again (although I do still feel precious about those perfect pink Chanel shoes), gathered together Scott and Melinda, David's best friend, to be our witnesses and photographers, and everybody took Friday off work. Melinda wanted me to have a tiny bit of tradition, so she brought me something borrowed (a brooch), and I pinned it through the blue ribbon I'd woven around an armload of tumbling peonies.

IT'S BEEN MORE than fourteen years since we met, and David is never boring. In fact, he delights me every day. Yes, we're an old married couple, and the urgency of new lust has faded into the tenderness of trusting love. He has a way of making me feel safe and much stronger than I think I could be on my own.

I treasure him. He is the most dear part of my life.

Sometimes I Just Break

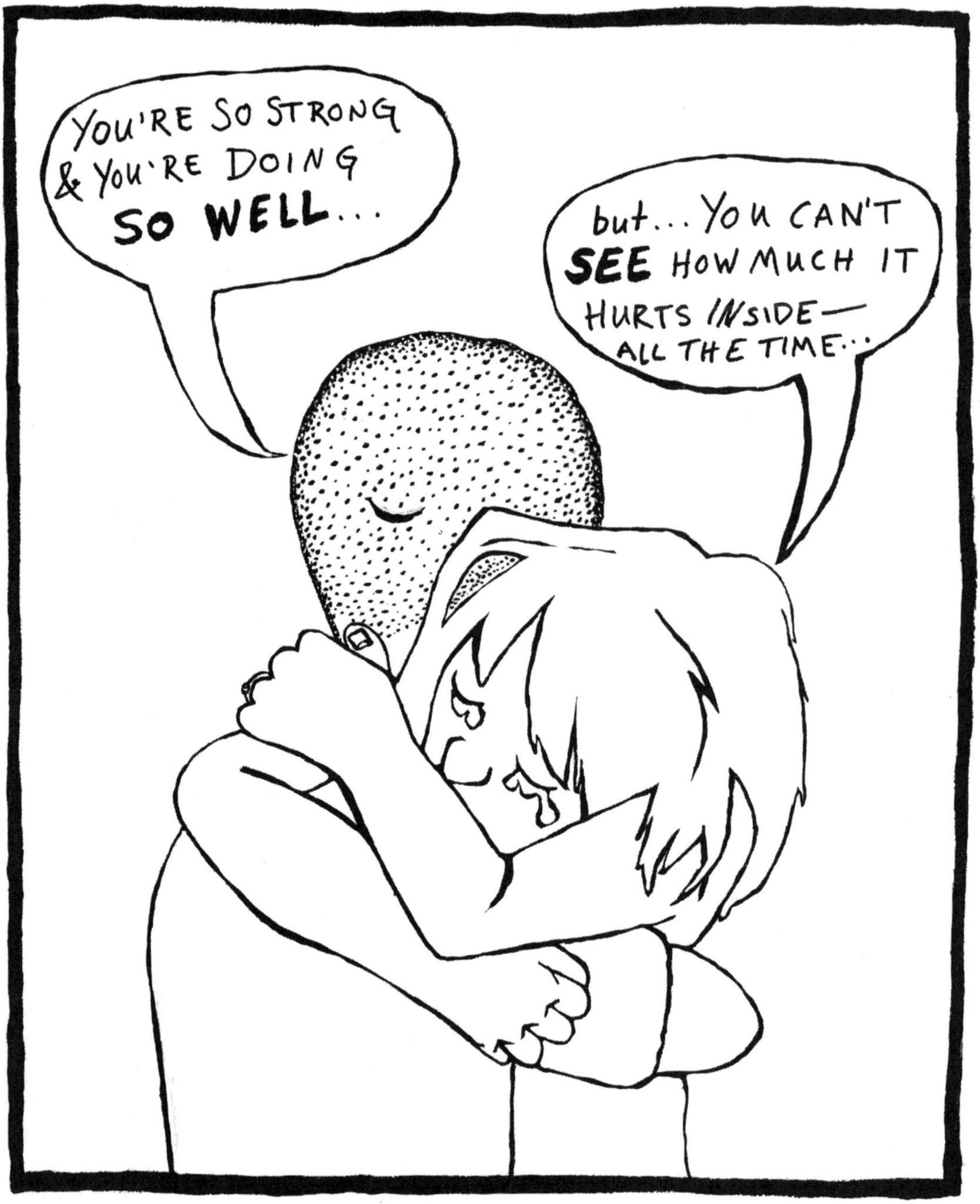
YOU'RE SO STRONG & YOU'RE DOING SO WELL...
but... YOU CAN'T SEE HOW MUCH IT HURTS INSIDE— ALL THE TIME...

Sometimes I Just Break

I try. I mean, I am always trying. Otherwise, I'd just stop.

It would be so easy, some days, to give up.

I want to be strong. I want to live fiercely and greedily, letting the fat run down my chin. And I don't want my cancer to be anybody else's problem.

Most days, I put up a good front. At least, I think I do. I'm not always sure how it looks from the outside.

Inside, there's pain. So constant that it can fade into the background like white noise. The dull ache of tumours in my bones, like a cavity writ large. Muscles, tense for weeks, knotted from straining to hold myself together. Stomach raw from pills. Hands gnarled into arthritic claws.

And my heart? My heart is breaking every day in the most selfish way. All the things I want. The excruciating act of scaling back my dreams. Paring down my hopes for this life into three-month bites. Living the enormity of hope and the gut-churning fear that accompany every single scan.

But when I break, when I can't adhere to my own edges, when I shatter with the winds, David catches me. He is steady against the wracking, wretched storm of my tears.

I hold onto him for dear life, both of which are all I ever wanted, anyhow.

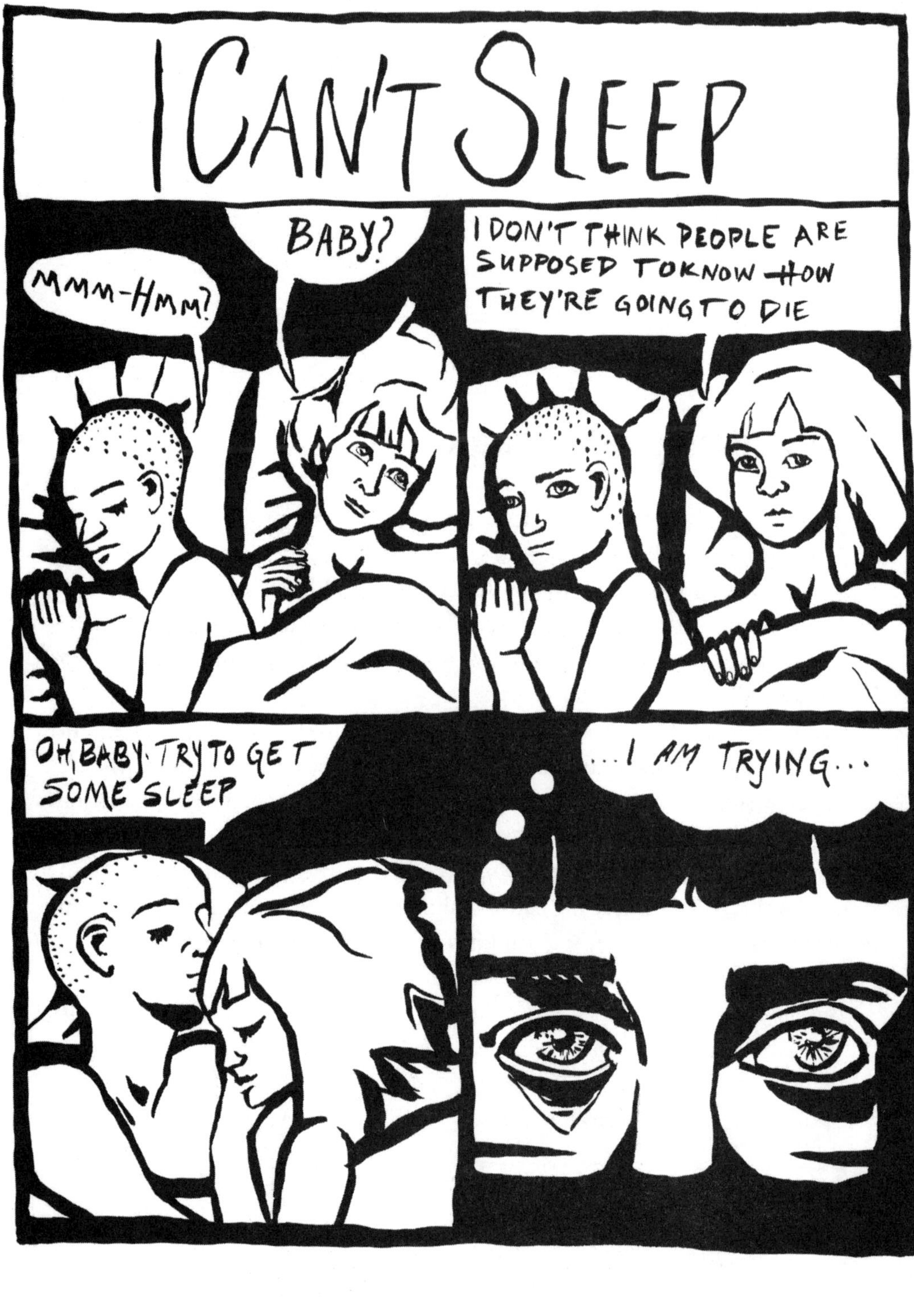
I CAN'T SLEEP
BABY?
MMM-HMM?
I DON'T THINK PEOPLE ARE SUPPOSED TO KNOW HOW THEY'RE GOING TO DIE
OH, BABY. TRY TO GET SOME SLEEP
...I AM TRYING...

I Can't Sleep

It's worst when I can't sleep.

That's when all my demon thoughts come to the surface. They love the dark. They swirl before my open eyes and blinking doesn't dim them.

Sometimes it gets so bad that I wake David up for a brief reprieve. He holds me, pets my hair, and for a moment the fears lose prominence. That's how powerful love can be.

But sometimes, I stop crying, and he goes back to sleep, and the demon thoughts come back stronger.

And I can't keep David up all night. He has to go to work through all of this, to maintain an even, competent manner.

While I slip deeper into the in-between spaces.

Family

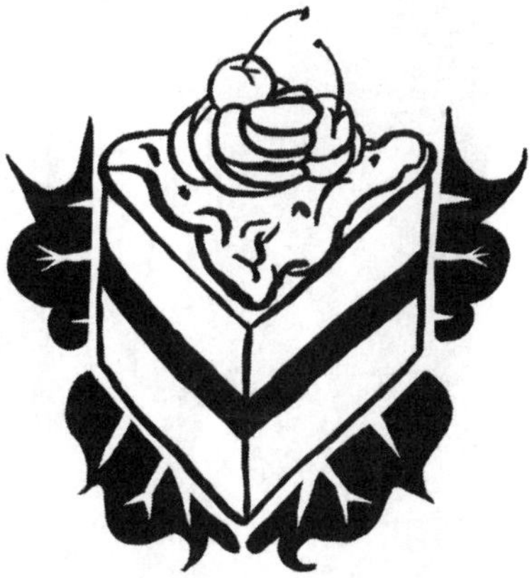

A MIXED-BAG INHERITANCE

The Women Of My Family

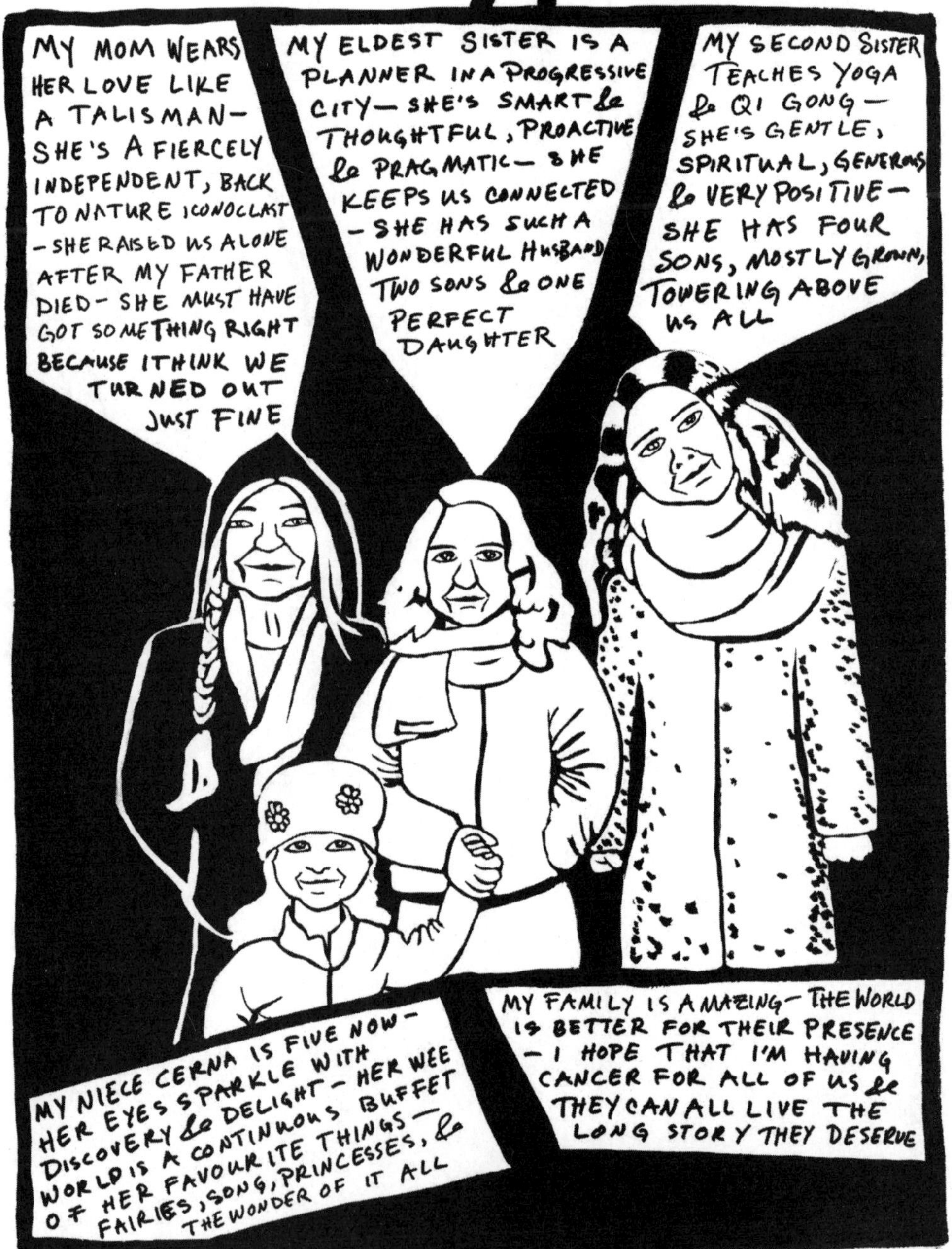

MY MOM WEARS HER LOVE LIKE A TALISMAN— SHE'S A FIERCELY INDEPENDENT, BACK TO NATURE ICONOCLAST —SHE RAISED US ALONE AFTER MY FATHER DIED— SHE MUST HAVE GOT SOMETHING RIGHT BECAUSE I THINK WE TURNED OUT JUST FINE
MY ELDEST SISTER IS A PLANNER IN A PROGRESSIVE CITY— SHE'S SMART & THOUGHTFUL, PROACTIVE & PRAGMATIC— SHE KEEPS US CONNECTED —SHE HAS SUCH A WONDERFUL HUSBAND TWO SONS & ONE PERFECT DAUGHTER
MY SECOND SISTER TEACHES YOGA & QI GONG— SHE'S GENTLE, SPIRITUAL, GENEROUS & VERY POSITIVE— SHE HAS FOUR SONS, MOSTLY GROWN, TOWERING ABOVE US ALL
MY NIECE CERNA IS FIVE NOW— HER EYES SPARKLE WITH DISCOVERY & DELIGHT— HER WEE WORLD IS A CONTINUOUS BUFFET OF HER FAVOURITE THINGS— FAIRIES, SONG, PRINCESSES, & THE WONDER OF IT ALL
MY FAMILY IS AMAZING— THE WORLD IS BETTER FOR THEIR PRESENCE —I HOPE THAT I'M HAVING CANCER FOR ALL OF US & THEY CAN ALL LIVE THE LONG STORY THEY DESERVE

The Women of My Family

Judaism is matrilineal, passing the family line through the mother, but my family took it a step beyond. For generations, only girls were born. My two sisters and I were born to my mother, who had only a sister. Their mother was one of four girls, and their mother one of three. And these are strong women, women who knew that they could accomplish anything they set their minds to, long before society began to smile on female ambition.

I can track my family back as far as I can our cancer. Everything before is lost to the ages.

MY MOTHER WAS left alone to raise three small girls on the hippie homestead she'd built with my father, who wanted to be a farmer. I barely remember the two years I was alive before my father died. For all intents and purposes, I was born to a family of women.

Our house was mercurial. One moment, shouting kids and slamming doors; the next, we were all peacefully reading in our rooms.

I'm the youngest, so I was always playing catch-up, reading books I didn't quite understand, trying to decode some joke that I knew was about sex (another idea that I didn't understand). It's the lot of the youngest to feel left out.

Keira, my middle sister, tried hard to include me. She read me stories every day, let me play with her older friends, and spent time explaining things, if I wasn't too embarrassed to ask. She also broke all the rules, and they stayed broken, clearing the way for my relatively easy teenage years. Despite her disregard for authority, she graduated second in her class. It's hard to keep a smart girl down.

My eldest sister, Malu, seemed to do everything right, but it might just have been that she knew how to not get caught. She was always involved in sports and clubs. We didn't have a lot to talk about because she's six years older than me, and that's a big age gap when you're kids. But when I was a little bit older, she wanted to get to know me. She invited me to spend spring break with her at university, where I manned the bar, pouring simple drinks and feeling useful and older. She went away to West Africa with the Peace Corps while I was still in high school, but when she came home, I spent another spring break with her in Albuquerque, where she went to graduate school.

My mother is deeply empathetic. She feels everything palpably, like a storm that sweeps everything up in its swirling intensity. I don't know how she managed to subjugate her grief when her husband and best friend, my father, left her by suicide. Somehow, she fed us and loved us and clothed us. Because no matter how huge her grief, her love was big enough to make her get up every day to care for us.

We all went on. We pushed forward into living. And when I look at my amazing family, I am so impressed with what everybody has done to find peace and a place in this world. Because tragedy is something we move through, and if we're lucky we find grace, joy, and light on the other side. I wish that for the people I love and am going to leave behind. I wish them a way through and a lightness on the other side of pain.

Since there's no way out for me, I hope I am the end of the line for cancer in my family. I hope my sisters, both older, are in the clear. I hope my mom doesn't have to go through the pain of having a sick daughter again. I hope my niece will never have to feel the anxiety that crowds my head, making me live in fear.

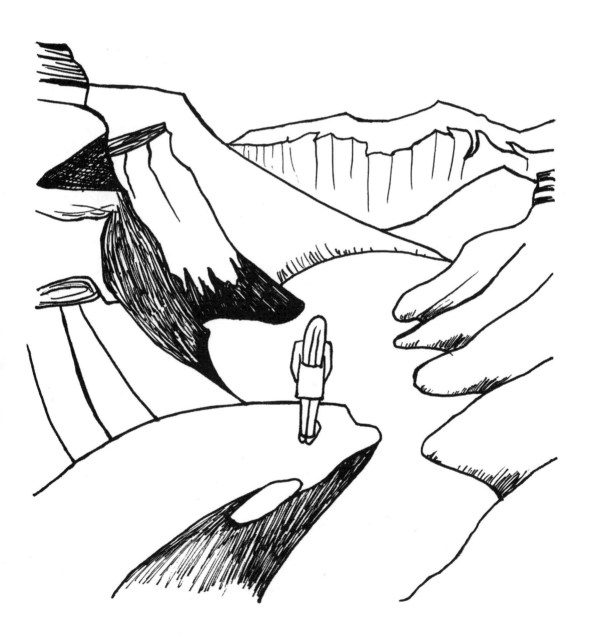

you're the Yin to my Yang
I WENT TO VISIT MY COUSIN
I HAVE SOME EXCITING NEWS!
I'M HAVING ANOTHER BABY!
I'M SO HAPPY FOR YOU!
& JEALOUS, IF I'M HONEST...
BUT I COULDN'T STOP THINKING ABOUT HOW SHE HAS LIFE GROWING INSIDE HER BODY WHILE DEATH GROWS IN ME...

You're the Yin to My Yang

My cousin Tova is three years younger than me. We're the closest in age among the first cousins, and we were really close growing up. The oldest generation was always confusing our names, both Hebrew words, only one letter off.

Tova is beautiful. She has our great-grandmother's big eyes, curly tumble of hair, and strong jawline. Her easy laugh is a window into her big heart.

Because her mother died so young, Tova's been watched closely for cancer her whole life. While doctors dismissed my concerns about early detection because the cancer in my family was at least two generations away, they took hers very seriously. Likewise, she thought long and hard before deciding to have children, for fear of leaving them without a mother. She was so sure that in our generation it was going to be her. She was afraid.

As time crept by, and life moved on, Tova was still here, still healthy, and she and her wonderful husband had a daughter with tumbling curls of her own, and later, a son.

And the universe laughs because it's not Tova but Teva who has cancer. My genes carry the family corruption.

My heart is near to bursting with the conflict of being so happy for her and so jealous. Of looking across the fence with longing for what could have been my life.

Sometimes, I torment myself with the wish that the cancer could end here, with me. I can't have children, but with the knowledge that this disease can jump generations, I am scared for my cousin's children, for my sister's.

Remembrances

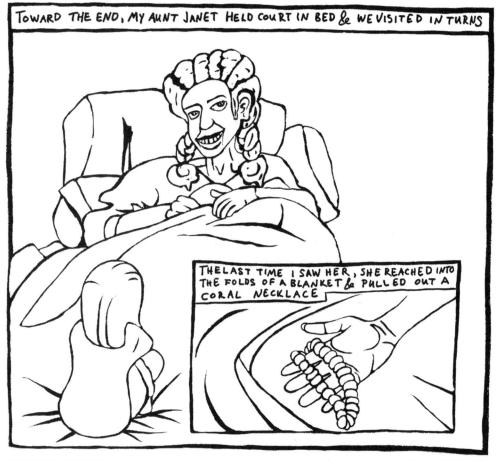

TOWARD THE END, MY AUNT JANET HELD COURT IN BED & WE VISITED IN TURNS

THE LAST TIME I SAW HER, SHE REACHED INTO THE FOLDS OF A BLANKET & PULLED OUT A CORAL NECKLACE

I WANT YOU TO HAVE THIS ...

WITH HER GAUZY NIGHTGOWN, SOFT CURLS, & THE FARAWAY LOOK IN HER EYES, SHE LOOKED LIKE AN ANGEL TO ME

Remembrances

Aunt Janet was my mom's little sister, her only sister. Her big bushy curls always made her seem slighter than she was, and she was a small woman with a wide, warm smile.

Janet was kind. She always made sure that the little ones like me felt included.

We spent holidays with Janet and her family, alternating between our house and theirs. It made us cousins close.

When Janet found out that she had breast cancer, it had already spread everywhere. She chose to forgo chemo, instead pouring her hopes into faith healers, eating strange foods, and wasting away.

Janet was only thirty-four when she died, leaving her husband lost in grief with two children too small to understand.

In the end, I remember her only in bed. The bed seemed extra vast to me because she was so frail—a radical mastectomy and cachexia had left her just a whisper of a woman. The wasting had left her features large, her neck drawn, her thick curls dwarfing her tiny body.

The last time I saw her, she gave me a coral necklace to remember her by. As if I could forget.

I understand now, though, the fear of being forgotten, of being erased. What is it that we leave when we go, except the impressions we've made on the people we've loved and who loved us?

BLINDED by the LIGHT

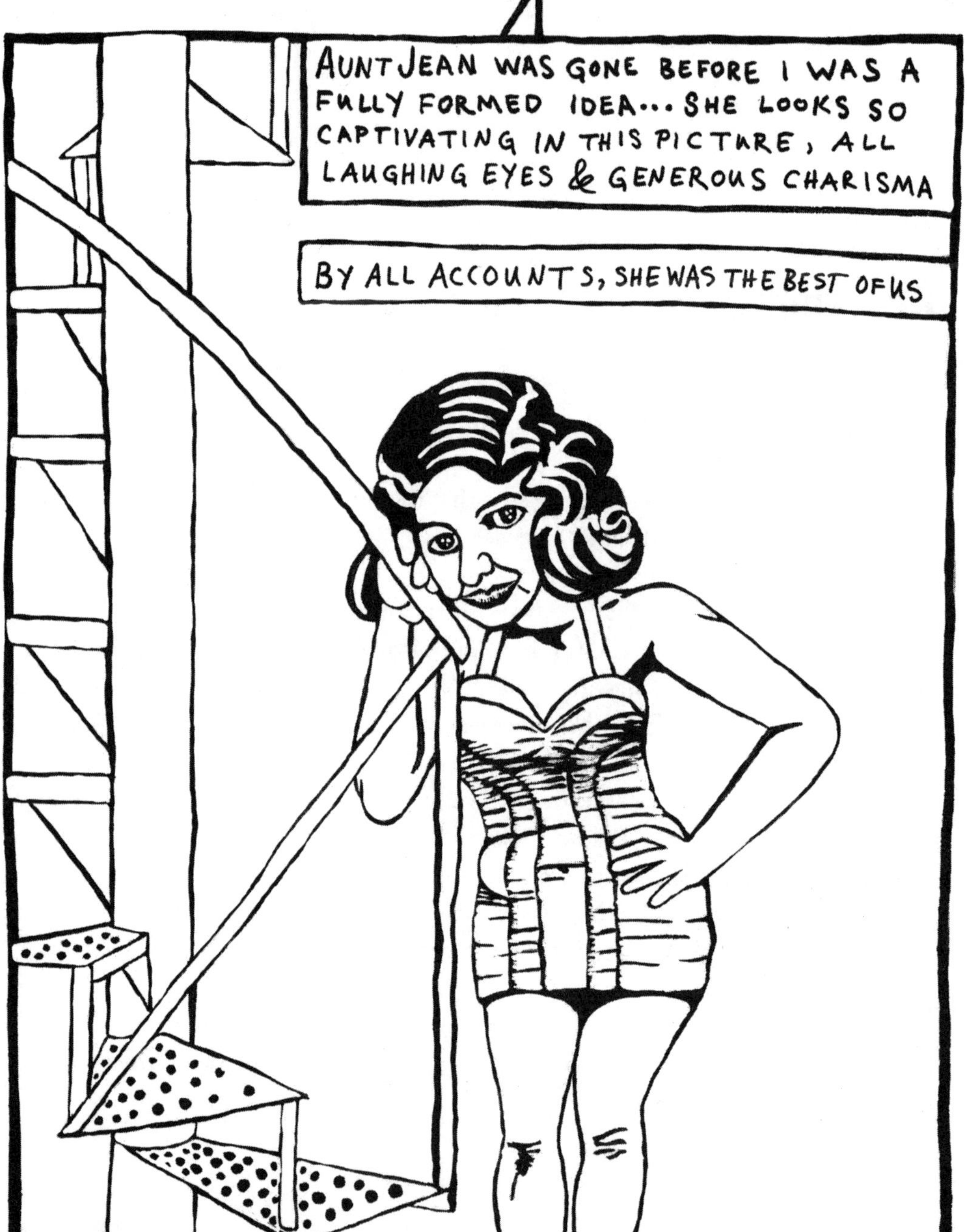
AUNT JEAN WAS GONE BEFORE I WAS A FULLY FORMED IDEA... SHE LOOKS SO CAPTIVATING IN THIS PICTURE, ALL LAUGHING EYES & GENEROUS CHARISMA
BY ALL ACCOUNTS, SHE WAS THE BEST OF US

Blinded By the Light

Kind. Patient. Accepting. Fun. Encouraging.

My great-aunt Jean looms luminous in everybody's memory.

She had a way of making you feel as if you were the most important person of all time. She did this for everybody, but that in no way cheapened the feeling. Rather, it demonstrated how giving she was of herself, her time, and her energy.

She just enjoyed people so much.

Jean was deeply involved in her family. She volunteered at her sons' schools, and by being present she was able to extend her glorious force of kindness to the children.

After my father died, when my mom was left alone with three little girls in a half-built house in rural Oregon, many people told her to give up and move. Not Aunt Jean. Ever encouraging and loving, she saw the loveliness of the rudimentary house and supported my mom in her choice to stay.

That was Aunt Jean: kind, accepting, and encouraging.

And when she died of metastatic breast cancer, she left an outsized void in the family.

In My Blood

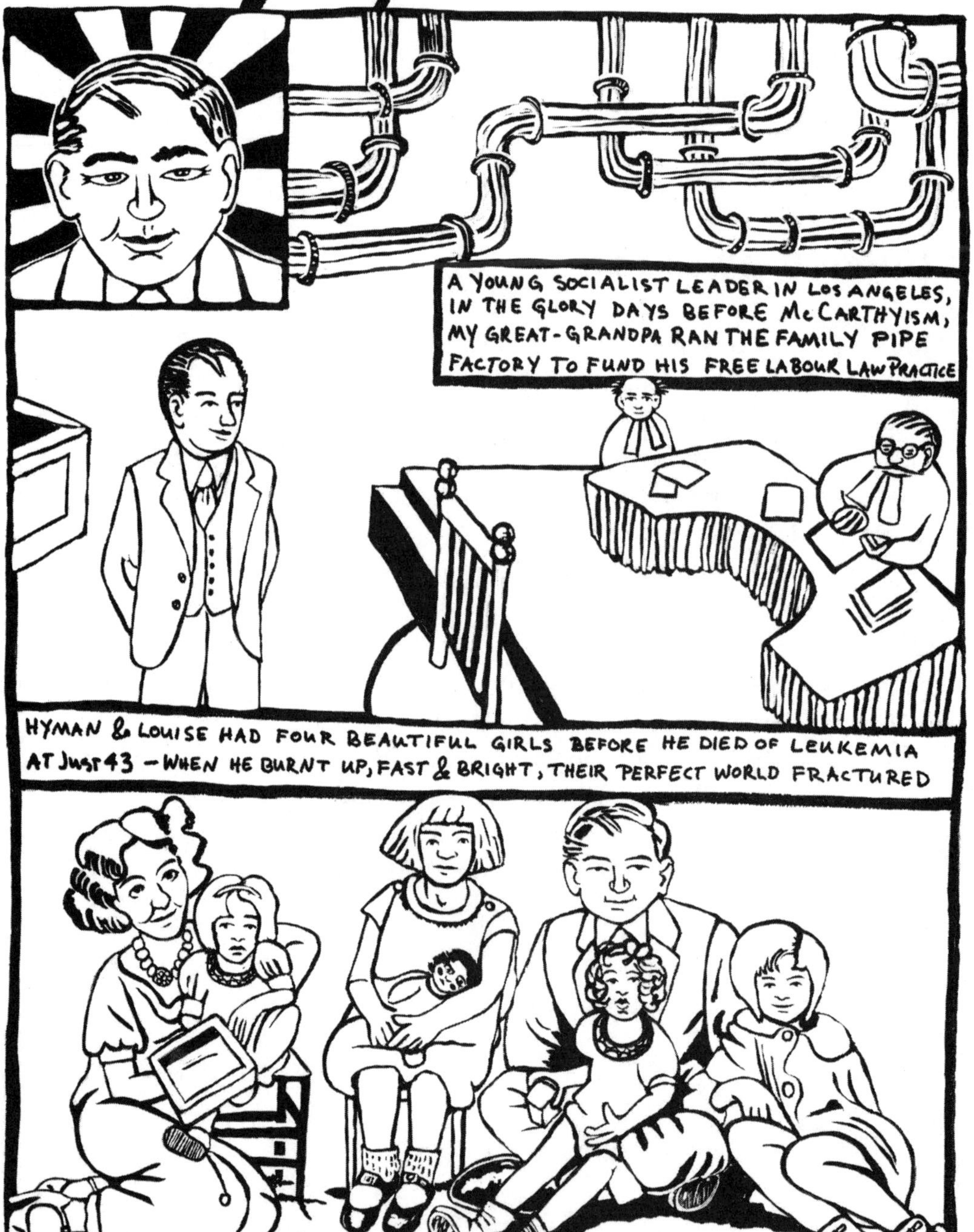
A YOUNG SOCIALIST LEADER IN LOS ANGELES, IN THE GLORY DAYS BEFORE McCARTHYISM, MY GREAT-GRANDPA RAN THE FAMILY PIPE FACTORY TO FUND HIS FREE LABOUR LAW PRACTICE
HYMAN & LOUISE HAD FOUR BEAUTIFUL GIRLS BEFORE HE DIED OF LEUKEMIA AT JUST 43 – WHEN HE BURNT UP, FAST & BRIGHT, THEIR PERFECT WORLD FRACTURED

In My Blood

This is the way I remember it. I'm sure some of it is wrong, as the folklore of families always is, but I cherish the stories of my memories. Moments that shine so bright and clear that everything else falls into darkness. Moments that only stay in focus when seen out of the corner of the eye. Moments I lived and moments that only live for me in story. The story of where I came from, the kinds of people we are, why. Stories of perseverance, joy, and loss. My family's stories.

My great-grandfather, Hyman Levin, was a mythical figure to me. He was a socialist lawyer in Los Angeles, ready and willing to live a life of service to make the world a better place.* In order to subsidize his labour law practice, he ran the family pipe manufacturing company, Kelly Pipe.

---

* My great-grandfather was very active at the time of Clarence Darrow, who is best remembered for his defense of teen "thrill" killers Nathan Leopold and Richard Loeb, and of substitute teacher John T. Scopes in the Scopes "Monkey" Trial. Hyman Levin did research for some of Darrow's early labour law cases, such as the show trial that convicted militant socialist leader Thomas Mooney of the San Francisco Preparedness Day Bombing of 1916 (a crime for which Mooney was eventually pardoned), and the trial of Iron Workers Union leaders the McNamara brothers, who stood accused of dynamiting the *Los Angeles Times*. Hyman's law partner, Job Harriman, was co-council with Darrow on the McNamara case, and it was to be his political undoing. Harriman carried the Socialist Labour ticket in 1911 with the popular vote and was on track to be elected mayor of Los Angeles.

Ever the idealist, Harriman believed the brothers innocent and was blindsided by a plea bargain negotiated by Darrow. Unfortunately for Harriman, the plea bargain was announced after the primary and before the general election, effectively tying Harriman's campaign to the McNamaras' guilt, allowing George Alexander to retake the mayoralty. The case ended Harriman's political aspirations, as he was unable to shake his association with the McNamaras enough to recover political capital in subsequent elections. It also contributed to the eventual collapse of the labour movement in Los Angeles, having eroded the credibility of the party's leaders.

Hyman Levin died of leukemia at forty-three, when my grandmother, the eldest of four girls, was twelve years old. It was his dedication to service, to the greater good, even against daunting odds, that inspired little Ruth Levin to live her life in the light.

BUT HOW DOES Hyman's cancer fit into the pattern of disease in my family? It wasn't a reproductive cancer, but it hit him when he was young, and it snuffed out his promise, shattering the idyllic world he and my great-grandmother had built.

There's so much we don't know about genetic cancer. I've had all available blood tests, and we are no closer to understanding why my family gets cancer. An outlier among the rest of our reproductive cancers, Hyman's cancer is linked to the rest of ours by the fact that it cut him down in his prime, just as he was on the verge of his greatest accomplishments.

The best I can hope is that my genes have contributed to the greater scientific investigation, that they might help somebody to zero in on an answer.

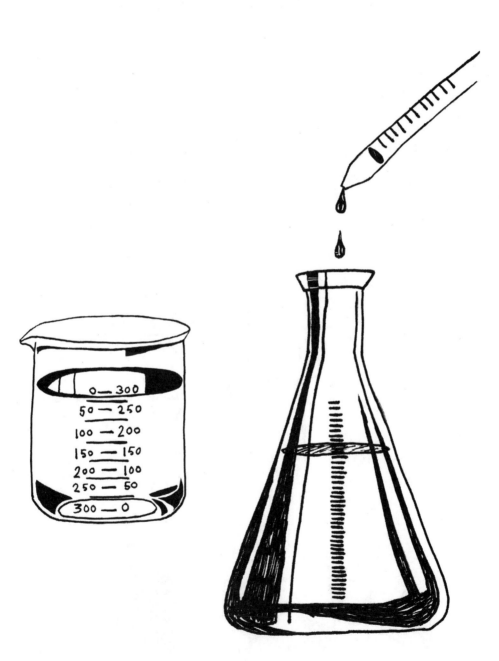

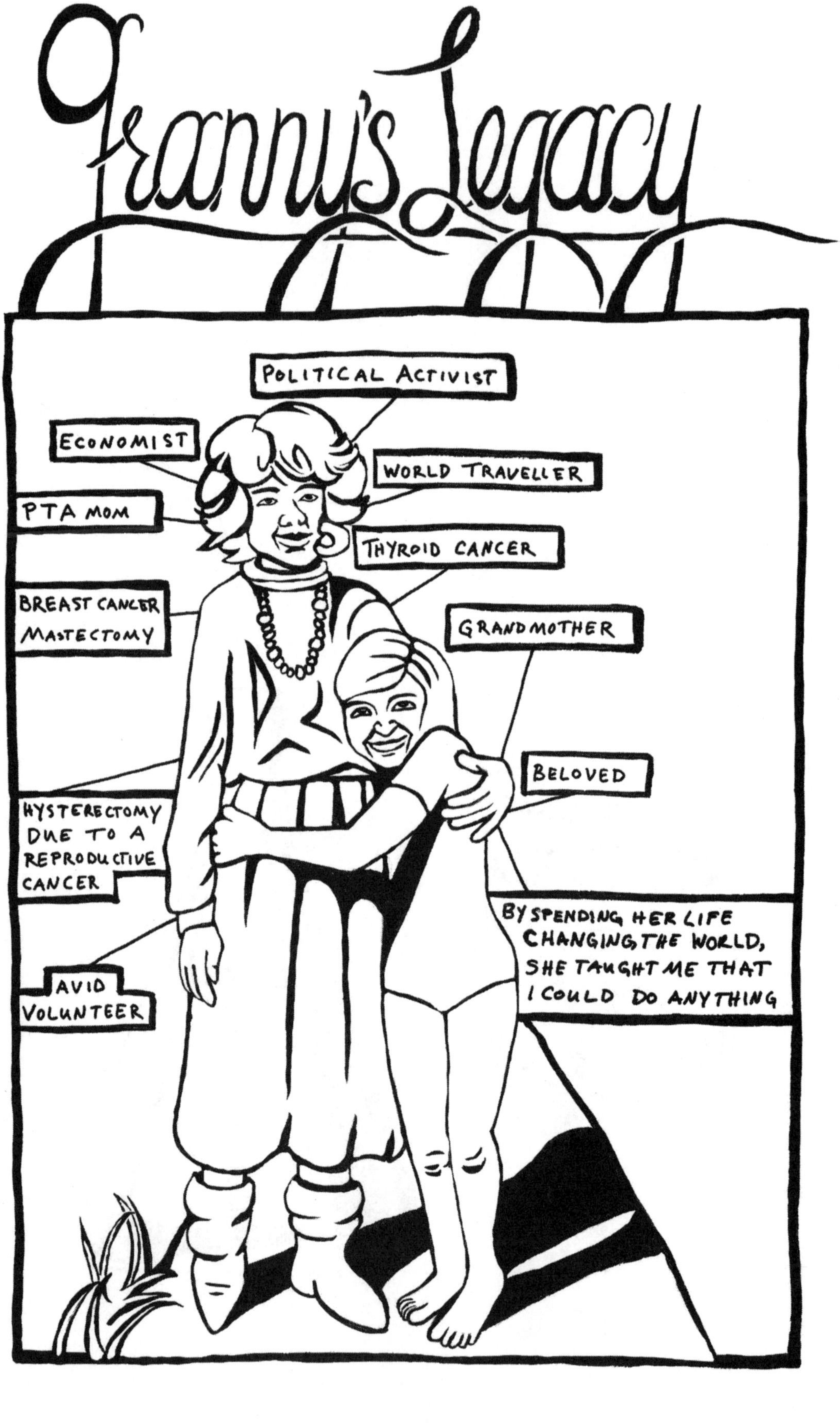
Granny's Legacy
POLITICAL ACTIVIST
ECONOMIST
WORLD TRAVELLER
PTA MOM
THYROID CANCER
BREAST CANCER MASTECTOMY
GRANDMOTHER
BELOVED
HYSTERECTOMY DUE TO A REPRODUCTIVE CANCER
BY SPENDING HER LIFE CHANGING THE WORLD, SHE TAUGHT ME THAT I COULD DO ANYTHING
AVID VOLUNTEER

Granny's Legacy

Ruth Levin March was a Stanford economist. When I was a little kid and I didn't know what economics were, I thought she'd majored in home economics at university, which was strange to me because she wasn't the sort of woman who baked a lot of cookies.

She was a tireless campaigner for the greater good, a lobbyist and organizer. Her work was diverse and interesting, and it took her from working with the International Olympics Committee to the United Nations, where she was the International Association for Volunteer Effort Liaison. Major accomplishments included successfully lobbying each U.S. state to recognize volunteer work as experience on job applications, campaigning for the GED high school equivalency program, and helping to develop the Head Start Program. Her various achievements were mentioned in the Congressional Record under pretty much every sitting president.

When she saw a problem, she also saw its solution and the path from here to there. I knew her as Granny.

Granny took me to volunteer for the first time, when I was eight, at the 1984 Summer Olympics in Los Angeles. I handed out bags to athletes, and they gave me their pins. She also gave us a very earnest board game called Volunteer. The game was modelled after Monopoly; in it, you went around and around the board, volunteering at the hospital or the animal shelter. To be honest, the game was no fun.

Granny wanted to show me how things worked, and she never wanted me to be shy about asking questions. When we had Indian food, she asked the owners to show me the oven where they cook the naan. On an airplane, she asked the flight attendants to take me into the cockpit to see how the plane was operated. If I had to use a washroom when we were travelling, she taught me to walk into the best hotel as if I owned the place, and nobody would ever question me. (This still works, by the way.)

When my sisters and I were old enough, she took us on trips. As each of us reached fourth grade, she took us to cities in the American northeast to teach us about our nation's early history, and then, a few years later, to Europe. The one-on-one time made each of us feel really special.

Granny was a world traveller before world travelling was widely done. She'd secure a guide and visit remote villages in Africa and South America. I have no idea what she ate or how money worked, but she sorted it out. By the time she died, of altitude sickness in La Paz, Bolivia, she'd been nearly everywhere but Antarctica. She had friends around the world, and she corresponded with them regularly. Her collection of folk art was amazing.

I always knew that Granny had survived cancer. She wasn't shy about letting me see her mastectomy scar when she was changing, and she was very candid with me that it was a scar from a cancer-related surgery, but I didn't realize just how much cancer she survived until I was diagnosed and asked for my family history. She had a hysterectomy when my mom was young because of a reproductive cancer; she had breast cancer; and, for the hat trick, she survived thyroid cancer.

But her legacy is so much more than cancer and the errant gene I carry. She made real changes, quietly, that improved life for millions of Americans. She has always inspired my best qualities, and now, she's my totem. Her memory is a potent reminder that, big and scary as this disease can be, I'm much more than my cancer, too.

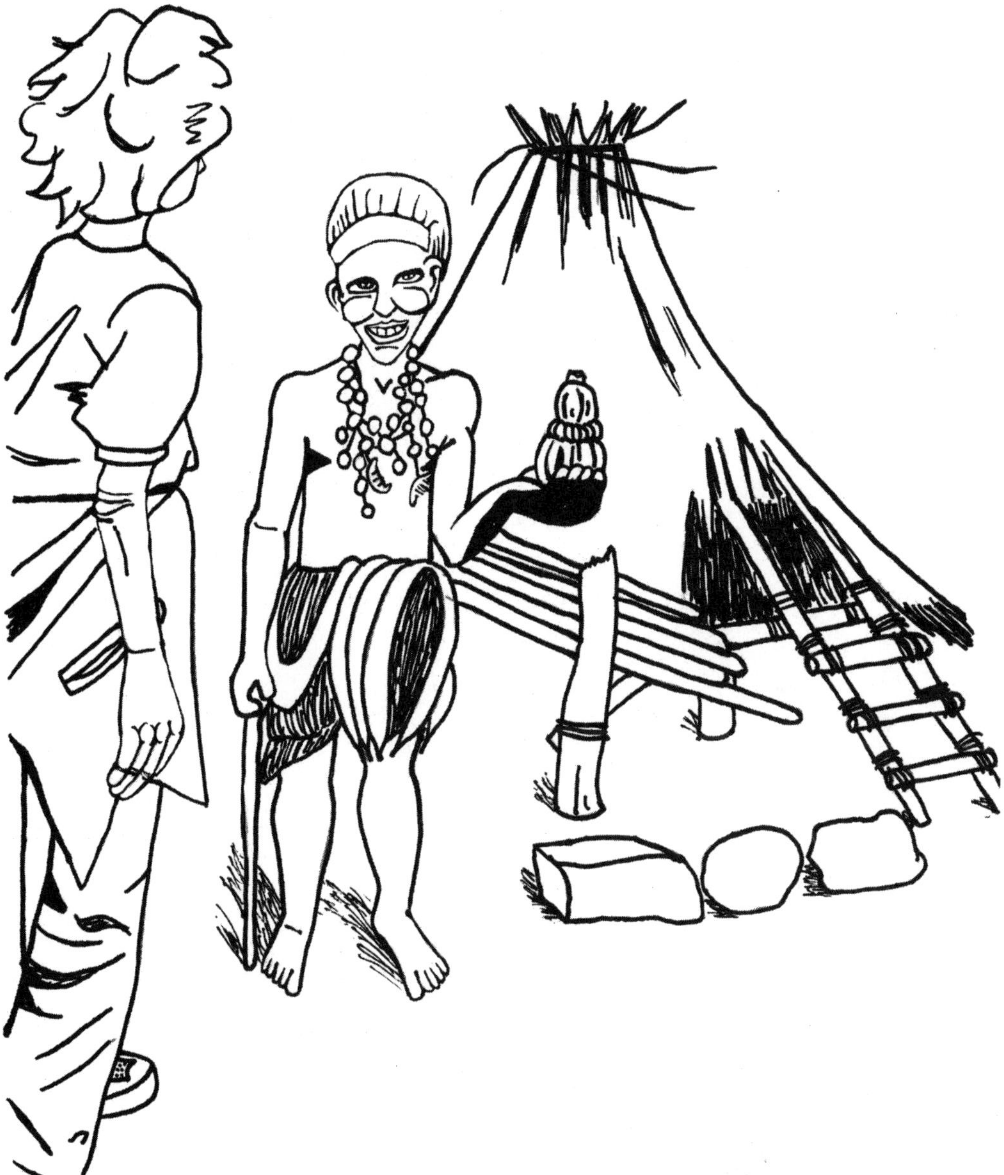

Society

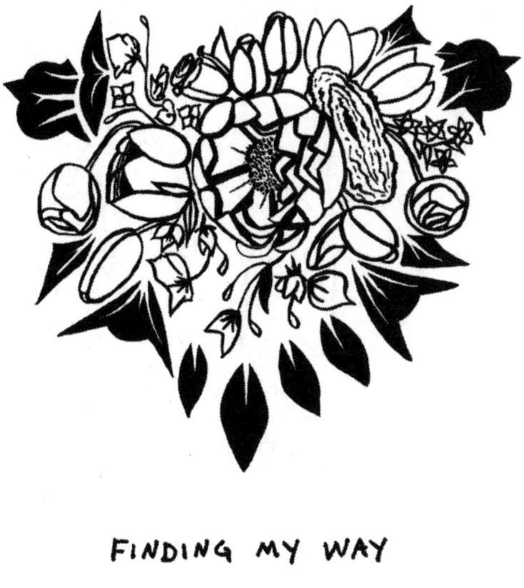

FINDING MY WAY

Invisibilities

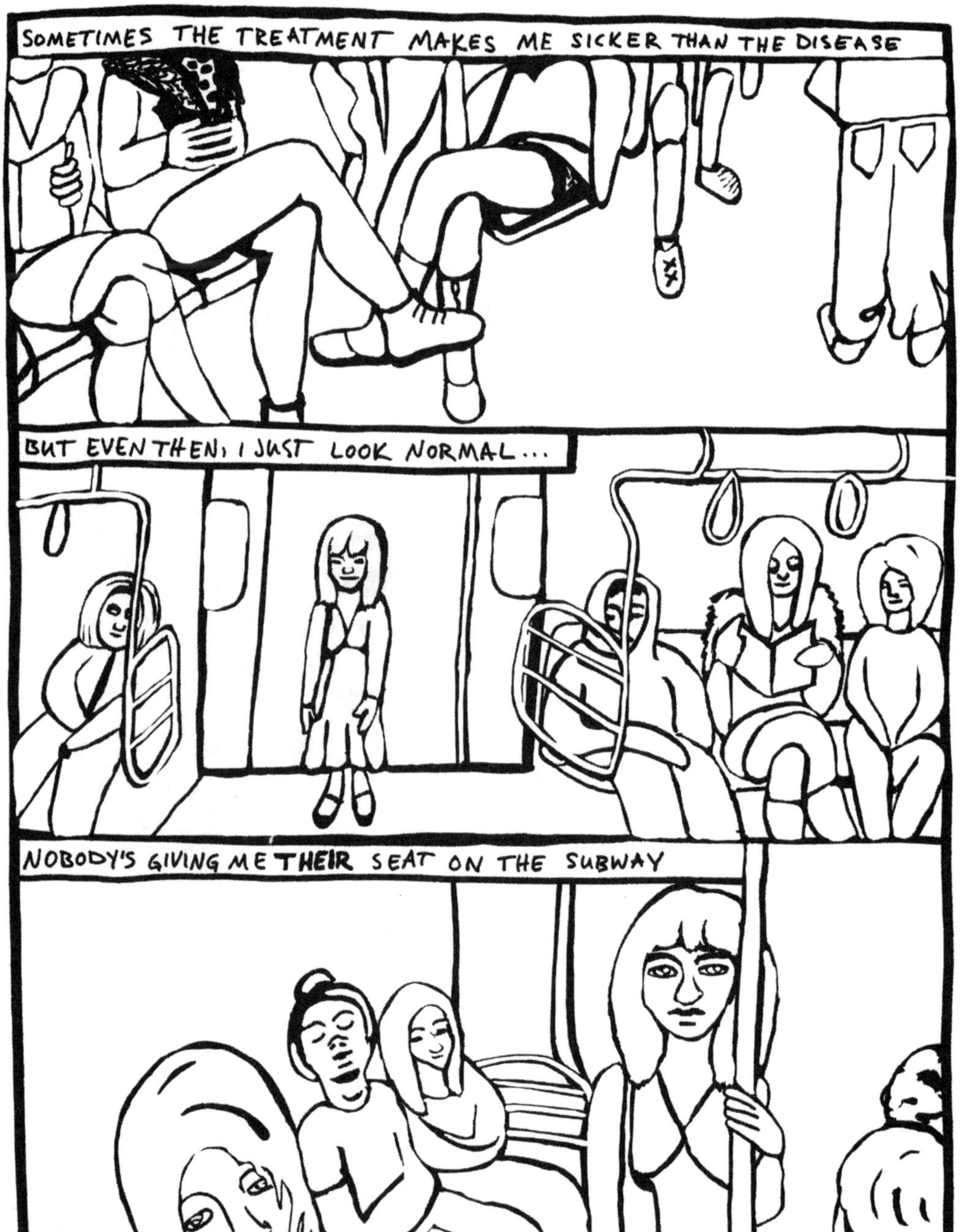
SOMETIMES THE TREATMENT MAKES ME SICKER THAN THE DISEASE
BUT EVEN THEN, I JUST LOOK NORMAL...
NOBODY'S GIVING ME **THEIR** SEAT ON THE SUBWAY

Invisibilities

Where does compassion begin?

What if suffering is invisible?

How can we be kinder?

Living with this disease has changed the way I look at the people around me. I wonder what pain they bear silently. I wish there was more that I could do. I think we all do, but we're taught to buck up, carry our lot.

Why do we find it so hard to ask for help? Once, I did ask for a seat on the subway. I was weak and sick and on the way to the hospital. I know that I looked fine, but I could hardly stand. The words were barely out of my mouth and a woman was on her feet. It probably made her happy to have helped somebody in distress.

So why did I feel guilty the entire ride?

Where does self-compassion begin?

The Incremental Erosion Of My Independence

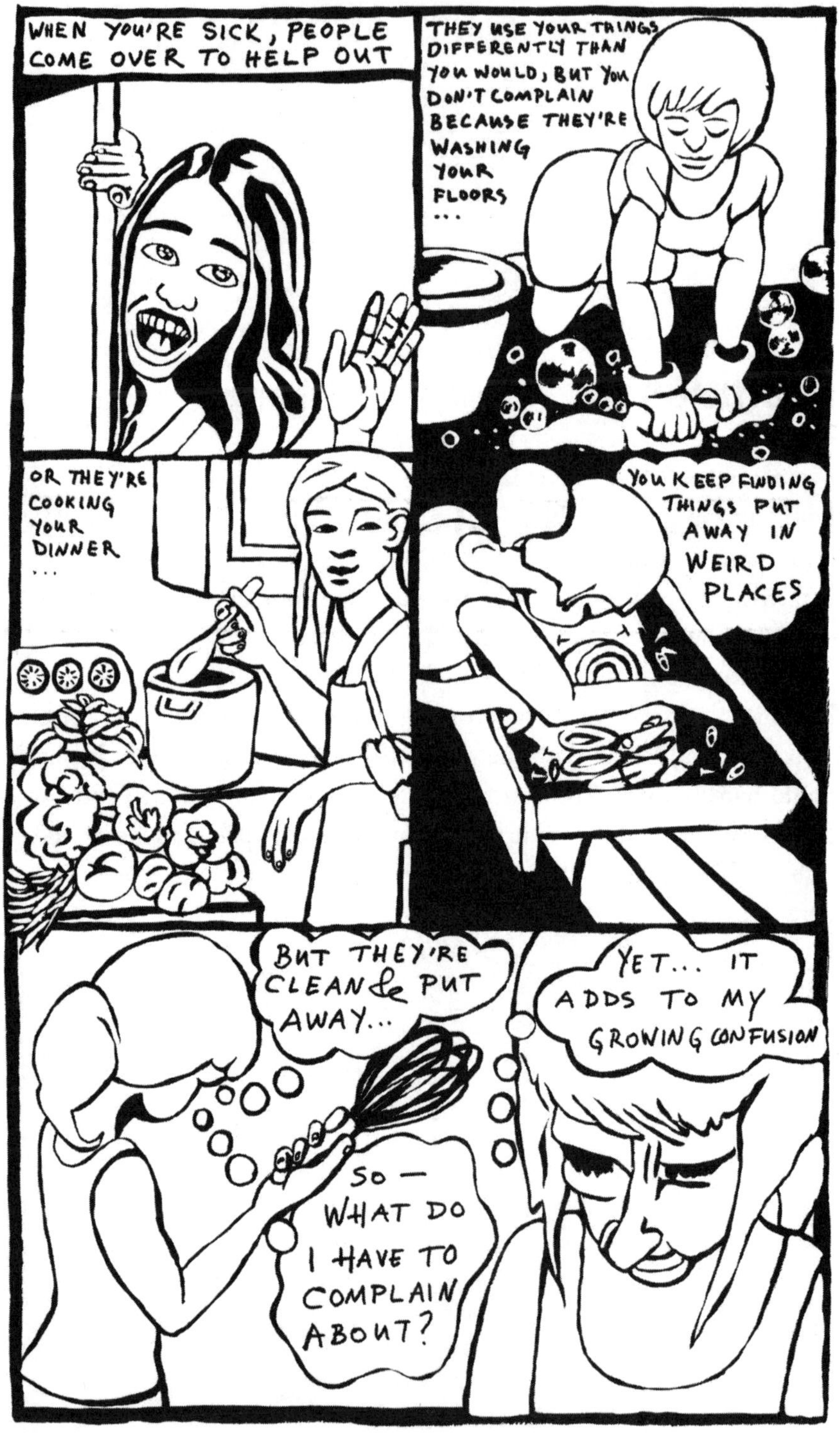
WHEN YOU'RE SICK, PEOPLE COME OVER TO HELP OUT
THEY USE YOUR THINGS DIFFERENTLY THAN YOU WOULD, BUT YOU DON'T COMPLAIN BECAUSE THEY'RE WASHING YOUR FLOORS ...
OR THEY'RE COOKING YOUR DINNER ...
YOU KEEP FINDING THINGS PUT AWAY IN WEIRD PLACES
BUT THEY'RE CLEAN & PUT AWAY...
SO — WHAT DO I HAVE TO COMPLAIN ABOUT?
YET... IT ADDS TO MY GROWING CONFUSION

The Incremental Erosion of My Independence

These days, I have lots of friends who know how to get into my house.

Sometimes they water my garden, do my dishes, wash the floors.

I'm very lucky to have this kind of support, especially living so far from my family, as I do.

But when home is all you have, when your things are what grounds you, the gentle shifting of your belongings can be distressing.

I have touch points. Items that only I know where to put away. People guess and their guesses are logical. It always makes sense when I finally find what I'm looking for in a place I'd never think to keep it. But the changes in my environment confuse me.

I can already feel what it is to lose independence, to be reliant. I've never been good at asking for help. Maybe that's the cosmic joke: to break down my ego by forcing me, after all these years, to receive kindness from the people I love.

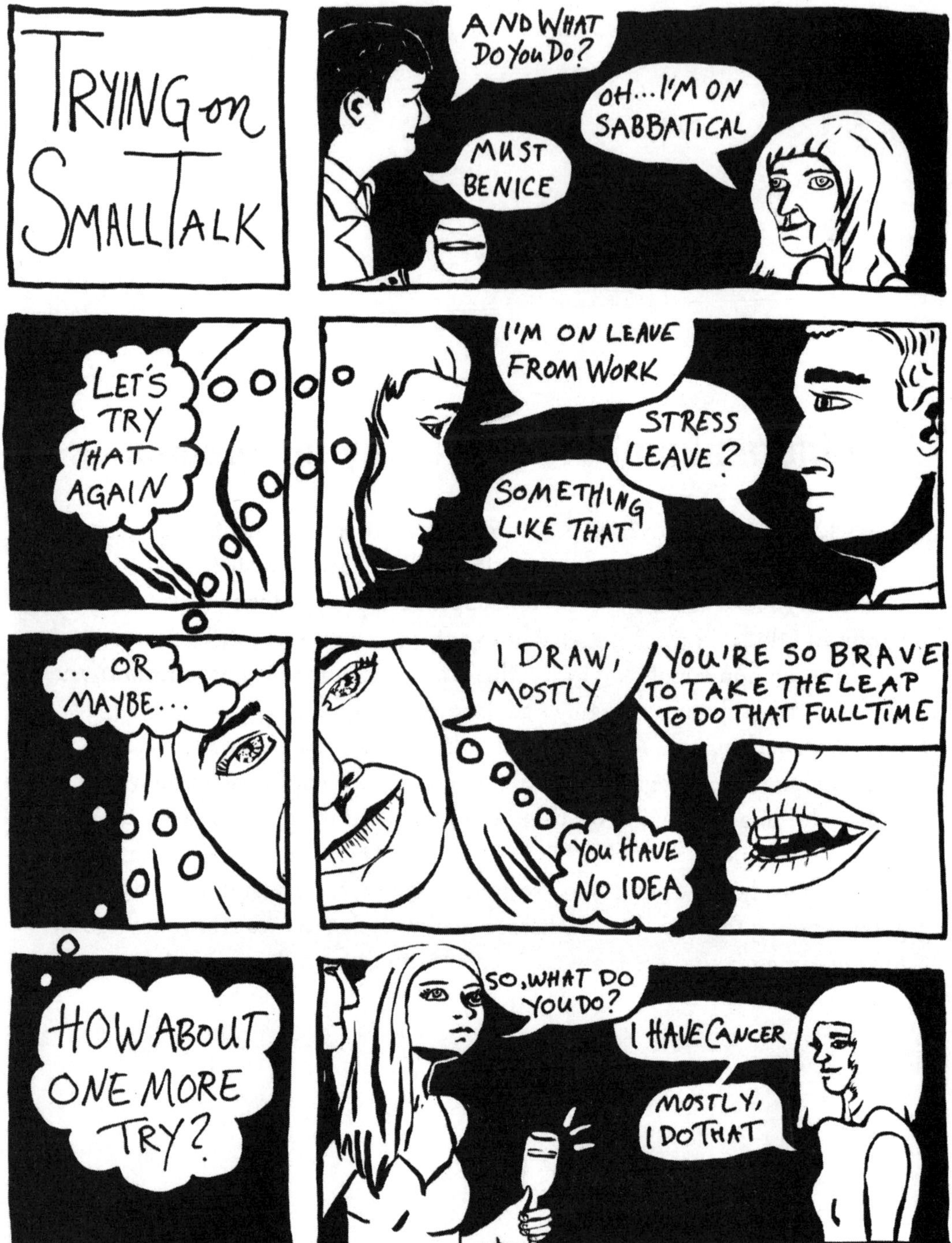
TRYING on SMALL TALK
AND WHAT DO YOU DO?
OH... I'M ON SABBATICAL
MUST BE NICE
LET'S TRY THAT AGAIN
I'M ON LEAVE FROM WORK
STRESS LEAVE?
SOMETHING LIKE THAT
... OR MAYBE...
I DRAW, MOSTLY
YOU'RE SO BRAVE TO TAKE THE LEAP TO DO THAT FULLTIME
YOU HAVE NO IDEA
HOW ABOUT ONE MORE TRY?
SO, WHAT DO YOU DO?
I HAVE CANCER
MOSTLY, I DO THAT

Trying on Small Talk

Small talk is easy when you have a job. If somebody asks what you do, you already have an elevator pitch at the ready. Or if you have kids, you can just go on about their latest cute discovery. I can see why. Kids keep your eyes wide to the world.

Small talk is a minefield when all you have to offer is cancer. It's touched everybody, but most people don't know how to talk about it or don't want to.

Except for a few people. There's a type of person desperate to talk about cancer: people who want to process the loss of a loved one.

And let's get real. The last thing this cancer patient wants to talk about is dead cancer patients.

And Then What?

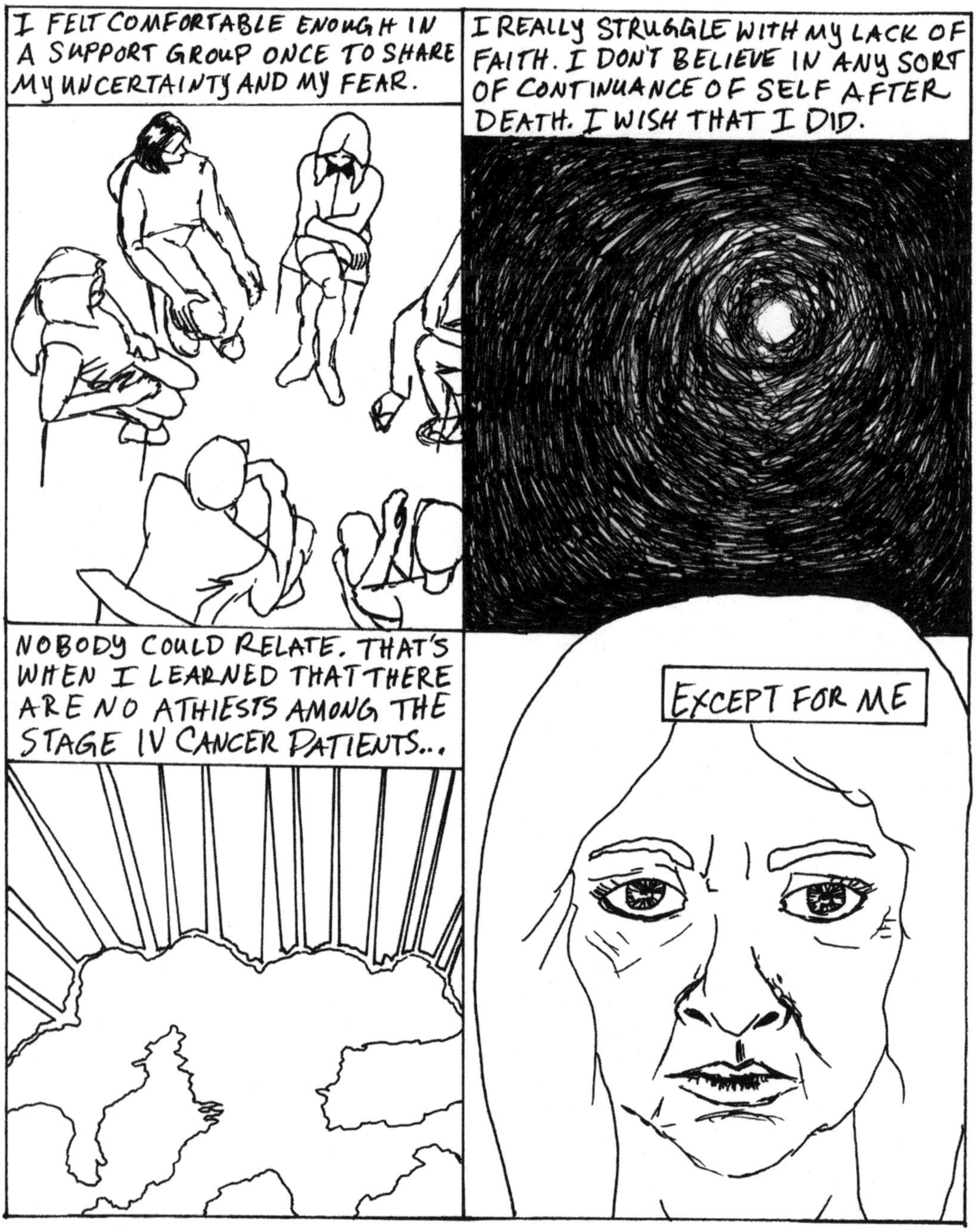
I FELT COMFORTABLE ENOUGH IN A SUPPORT GROUP ONCE TO SHARE MY UNCERTAINTY AND MY FEAR.
I REALLY STRUGGLE WITH MY LACK OF FAITH. I DON'T BELIEVE IN ANY SORT OF CONTINUANCE OF SELF AFTER DEATH. I WISH THAT I DID.
NOBODY COULD RELATE. THAT'S WHEN I LEARNED THAT THERE ARE NO ATHIESTS AMONG THE STAGE IV CANCER PATIENTS...
EXCEPT FOR ME

And Then What?

I've never believed in an afterlife, not really. I was raised with a mishmash of beliefs, a cherry-picked amalgam of spirituality and magic, cobbled together from family tradition and Eastern practices. And most of them just didn't take.

I mean, I love the way celebrating Jewish holidays connects me to my family, living and dead, and to a community that I belong to by birth, yet I know less about this religion than most theology students do. I love being Jewish. And I also loved the beautiful Sant Mat books my mom gave me to teach me about reincarnation and returning to the sea of love. Karma and mitzvahs are beautiful ideas, both of which encourage people to be kind to one another.

I do believe in kindness.

Yet in some way that I can't pin down or properly articulate, I believe in some sort of Earth magic, that there's something in the very fabric of our planet and the life on it that goes beyond the tangible, the visceral, and that can't be explained.

But mostly I believe in science, and try as I might I just don't believe that I will continue to exist after I shake off this mortal coil. I don't believe that there is a heaven waiting for me, and I don't believe that I will be reincarnated, either as a lower form of life (come to think of it, I don't really believe that any form of life is higher or lower than any other) or as a more enlightened being. I don't think that Teva, as we all know her, gets to continue as an entity when the energy of her body has transferred into some other kind of energy here on Earth.

Yet here I am, facing the likelihood of my early demise, and I want, want, want to believe in something more, but I can't. I just can't.

I once heard a kid describe what he believed happened when we die: he said everybody gets what they believe in.

But what if you can't make yourself believe?

And yet, every time somebody tells me that they're praying for me, I say thank you, and I mean it. I can't explain how it is that I believe that this will help or the depth of gratitude that I feel for the people who keep me in their thoughts in those personal sacred moments.

I tried, once, to open up to a group that I thought might understand, a circle of my peers living with metastatic cancer. They looked at me with sad, kind eyes, but no recognition. Not one arm went up to say, yes, I'm scared too, because I don't know how to believe.

Atheism doesn't sit well with a terminal diagnosis.

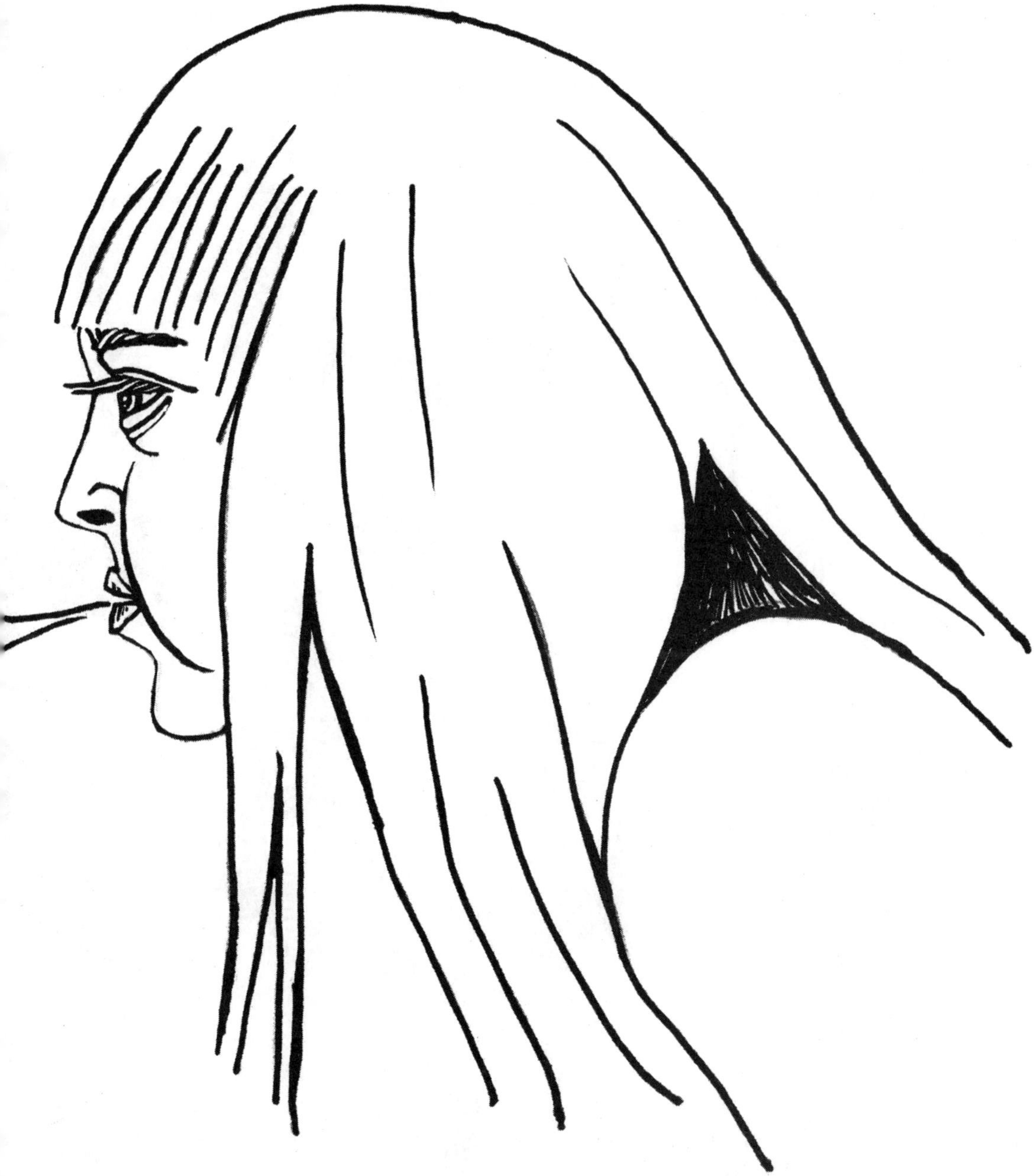

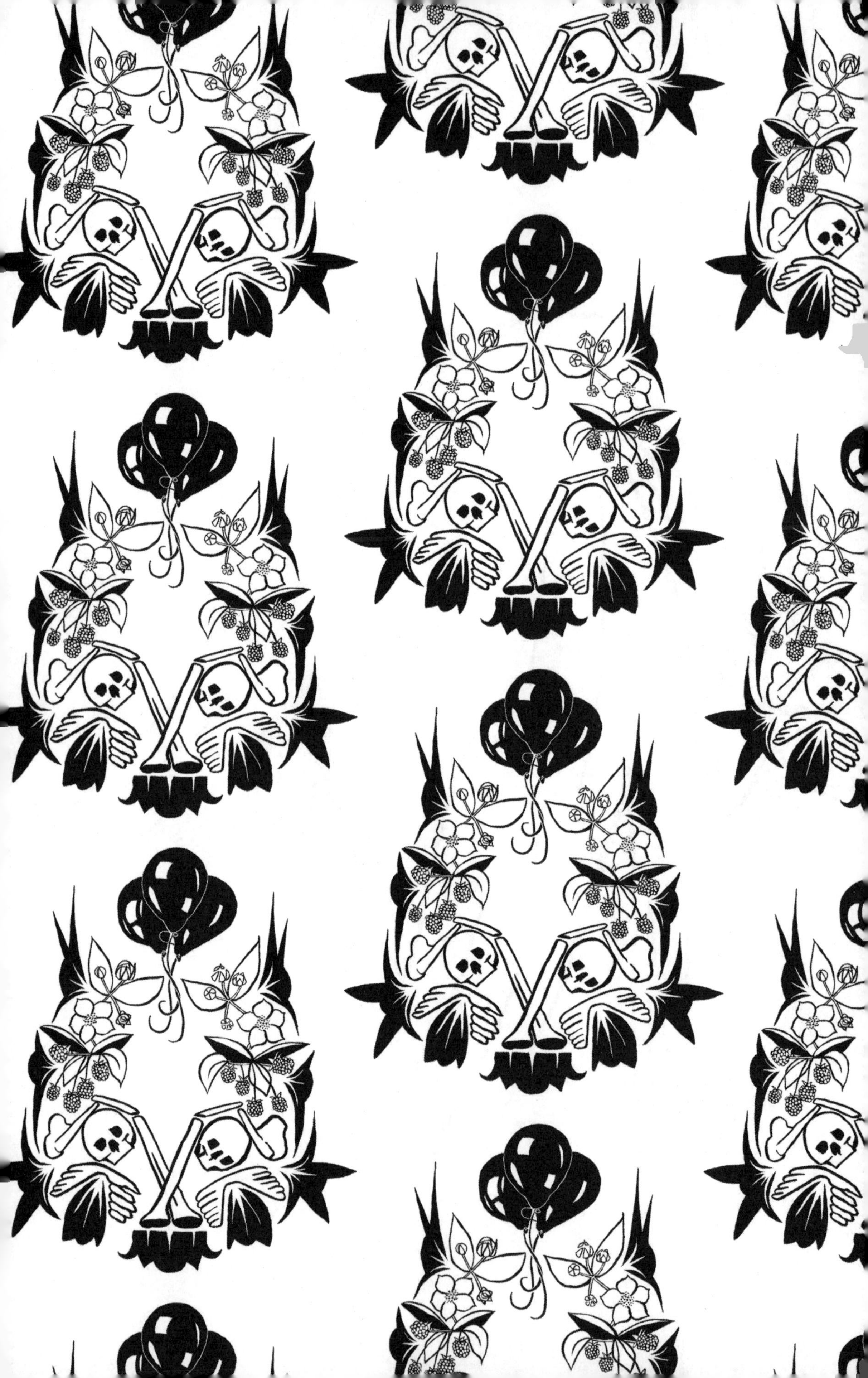

PART THREE

Hopes

IF WISHES WERE HORSES

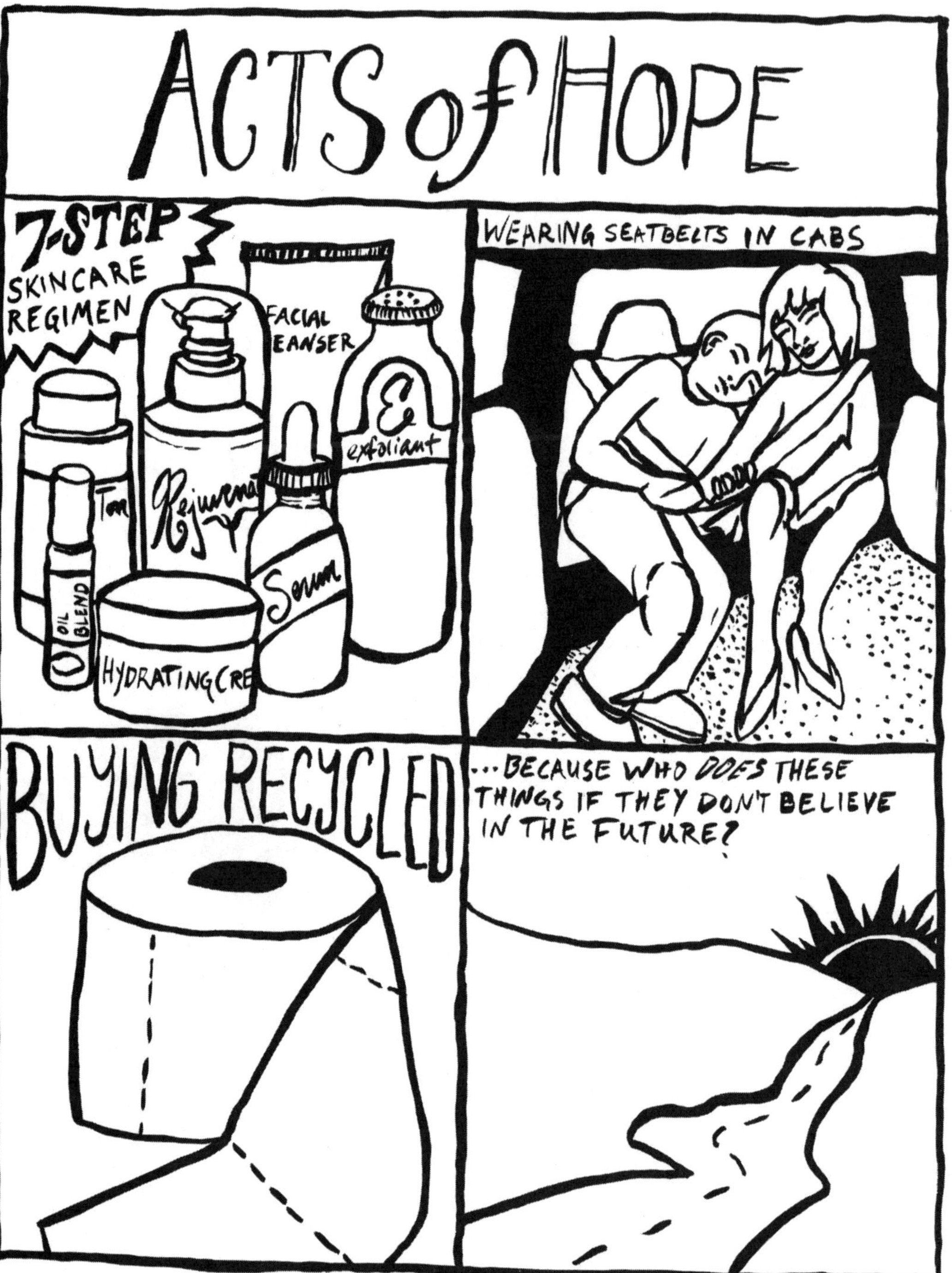
ACTS of HOPE
7-STEP SKINCARE REGIMEN
FACIAL CLEANSER
Exfoliant
Toner
Rejuvenate
Serum
OIL BLEND
HYDRATING CREAM
WEARING SEATBELTS IN CABS
BUYING RECYCLED
...BECAUSE WHO DOES THESE THINGS IF THEY DON'T BELIEVE IN THE FUTURE?

Acts of Hope

Living with cancer requires hope.

I hope that I can stay alive for science to find a way to sustain me for the long term, even to cure my cancer. That's why I participate in clinical trials. I want to help the doctors and researchers get there faster.

I hope to spend years with the people I love: my amazing husband, my wonderful family, and my beloved friends.

I am chock full of hope, mostly because I need it to get through every single day.

Hope means that I can go on.

The Snowball Fight

ONE TIME, AUBREY & I HAD A SUMMER SNOWBALL FIGHT

WE RIPPED THE BIG, SOFT BALLS OF FLOWERS OFF THE BUSH

& RAN THROUGH THE YARD THROWING THEM BACK & FORTH

UNTIL THE BUSH WAS EMPTY, FLOWERS BROKEN ON THE GRASS

The Snowball Fight

I met Aubrey when we were babies. A year younger, and never as responsible, I've always been more of a baby than him, but he's been able to overlook it for the nearly forty years that he's been my best friend.

We were the first generation of children growing up as hippies in a rural southern Oregon town, where our parents moved to live a dream of a simpler life. We could play for hours, catching giant bullfrog tadpoles in Aubrey's pond or making chains of daisies in the field at my house. We spent our summers outside.

Magic was alive and everything was possible.

Aubrey's mom had a beautiful garden, with flowers forever. Lush, blooming bushes softened the edges of the house, all tumbling into green.

Once (and only once) Aubrey and I had a summer snowball fight.

We ripped the big, soft flowers off the snowball bush and built up our ammo in piles of petals, then wound up our arms and threw them. The petals kissed us and slipped silkily to the ground.

Laughing open mouthed or through our teeth, we picked them up and threw them back, the gentlest war.

It took a long time for us to tire of this game. The bush was empty. Our munitions crushed and limp.

I KEEP FINDING my thoughts drifting back to the wide-open possibilities of my childhood.

The forests were alive with creatures, real and imagined: turtles on logs that jumped into the pond if we were too loud, spotted fawns glimpsed through trees and then a flurry of disappearing hooves, toadstool fairy houses on the lush and mossy forest floor. We were only constrained by the breadth of our imaginations.

I yearn to feel free like that again.

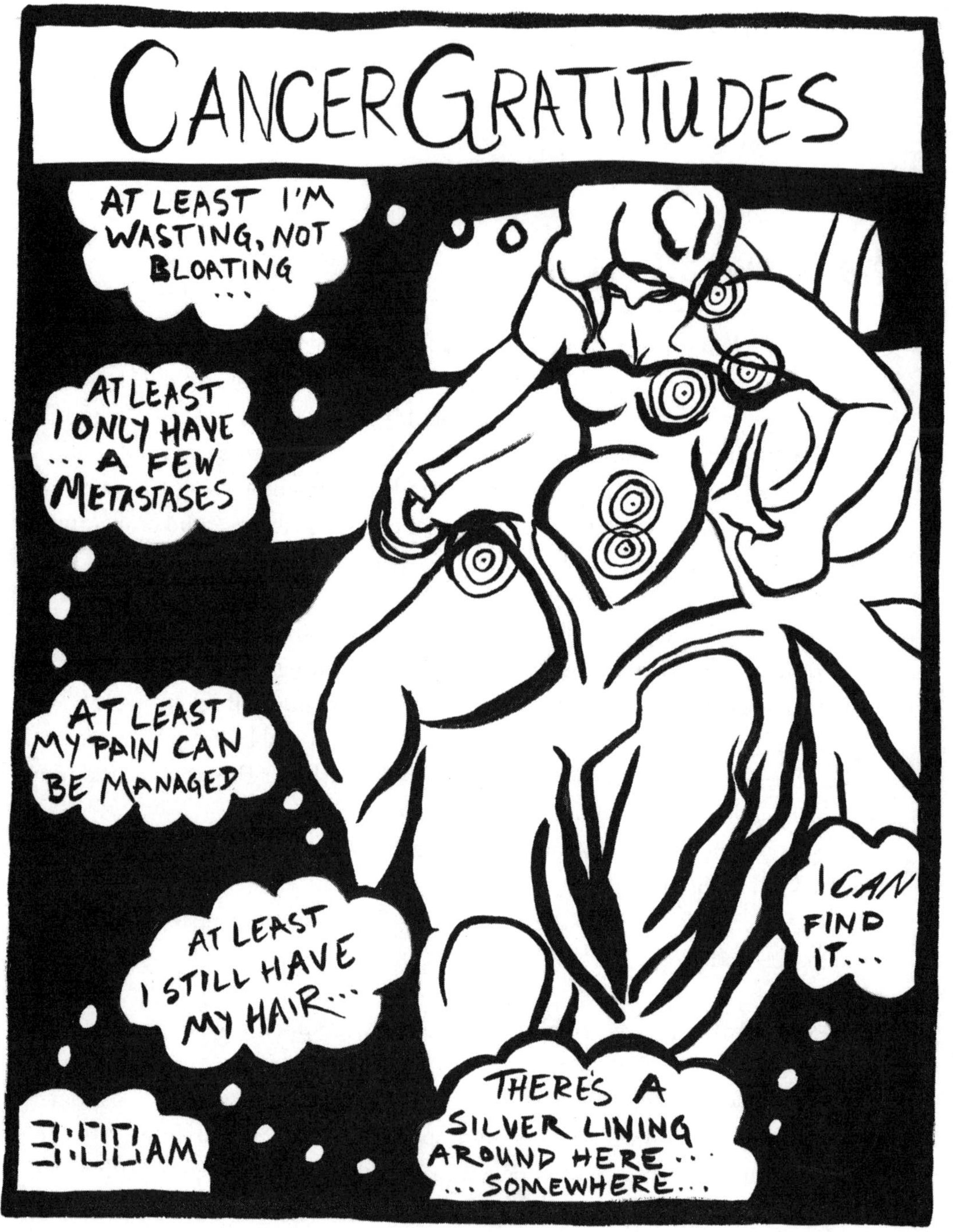
CANCER GRATITUDES
AT LEAST I'M WASTING, NOT BLOATING ...
AT LEAST I ONLY HAVE ... A FEW METASTASES
AT LEAST MY PAIN CAN BE MANAGED
AT LEAST I STILL HAVE MY HAIR...
I CAN FIND IT...
THERE'S A SILVER LINING AROUND HERE... ...SOMEWHERE...
3:00AM

Cancer Gratitudes

I have always been masterful at finding the silver linings.

Cancer can make that harder, but they're still there.

I keep needing to tell myself that, sure, I have incurable cancer that's going to kill me one day, but other people have it much worse. They might actually know when to expect death, whereas I can pretend that it's in the distant future. I dwell on the depths of agony that are still unknown to me, and I experience a shameful hint of *schadenfreude*.

So I lie awake and tell myself that it could be worse. And by the end, I think I believe it.

Mouthful Of Wishes

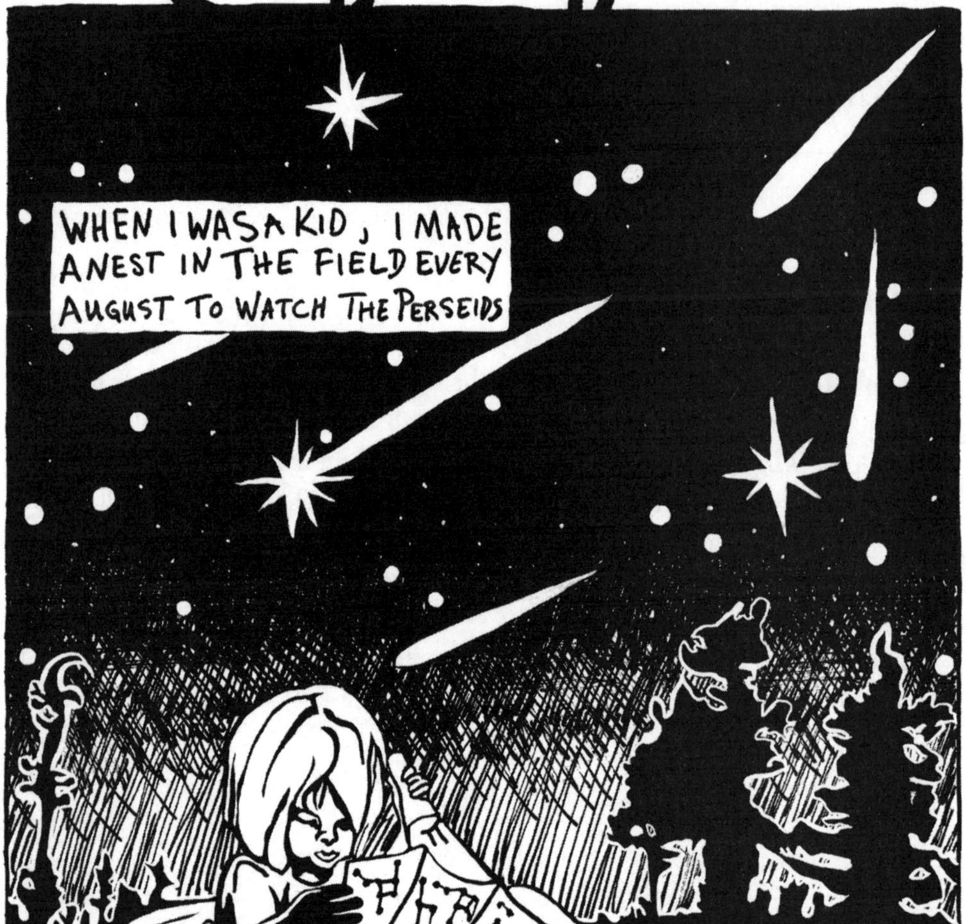

Mouthful of Wishes

I grew up in the fertile Williams Valley, between the Coast and Cascade Mountain ranges. My parents were a different kind of pioneer on the Oregon Trail: back-to-nature hippies, looking to make a new kind of life for their little family.

There was magic everywhere.

To get to my house, you drove and drove, first to tiny Williams, a town with no stoplights and a general store with a hitching post. Then you drove some more until you reached our gravel drive, cut out of a wall of blackberry bushes (not my favourite chore). Our house was set back into the trees, trees my parents planted to cool the house in the summer and break the wind in the winter.

In front of the house, we had an open fescue grass pasture. When we had horses, we'd thresh the grass into hay that would feed them all year round. Now the horses are gone, and I think my mom sells the hay back to the man who bales it.

Cut down, the field was a massive lawn under clear, open skies. The stars sparkled so brightly it hurt. Small and curious, I'd built a summer nest in the field, a bed that was also a fort. I dragged a blue tarp out, as a base, and then rebuilt my bed out of blankets and pillows, cushioned only by grass and earth. I brought out a flashlight, books, water, and snacks.

I had a star map, and I was going to learn it. I was going to learn everything.

I settled in for the month of August, which was the best month for stargazing because of the Perseid meteor showers that filled the sky with shooting stars. It was a game to me, trying to wish on all of them and not use the same wishes over and over.

Now, I would wish for only one thing.

I still make wishes every chance I get. I wish when the clock lines up to repeat a digit, but especially at 11:11. I wish when the clasp of my necklace slides to the front. I wish hard when I blow out my birthday candles. I'm not terribly superstitious, but I believe in the power of secret longing, the power of hope.

Fears

THEY DON'T JUST GO BUMP IN THE NIGHT

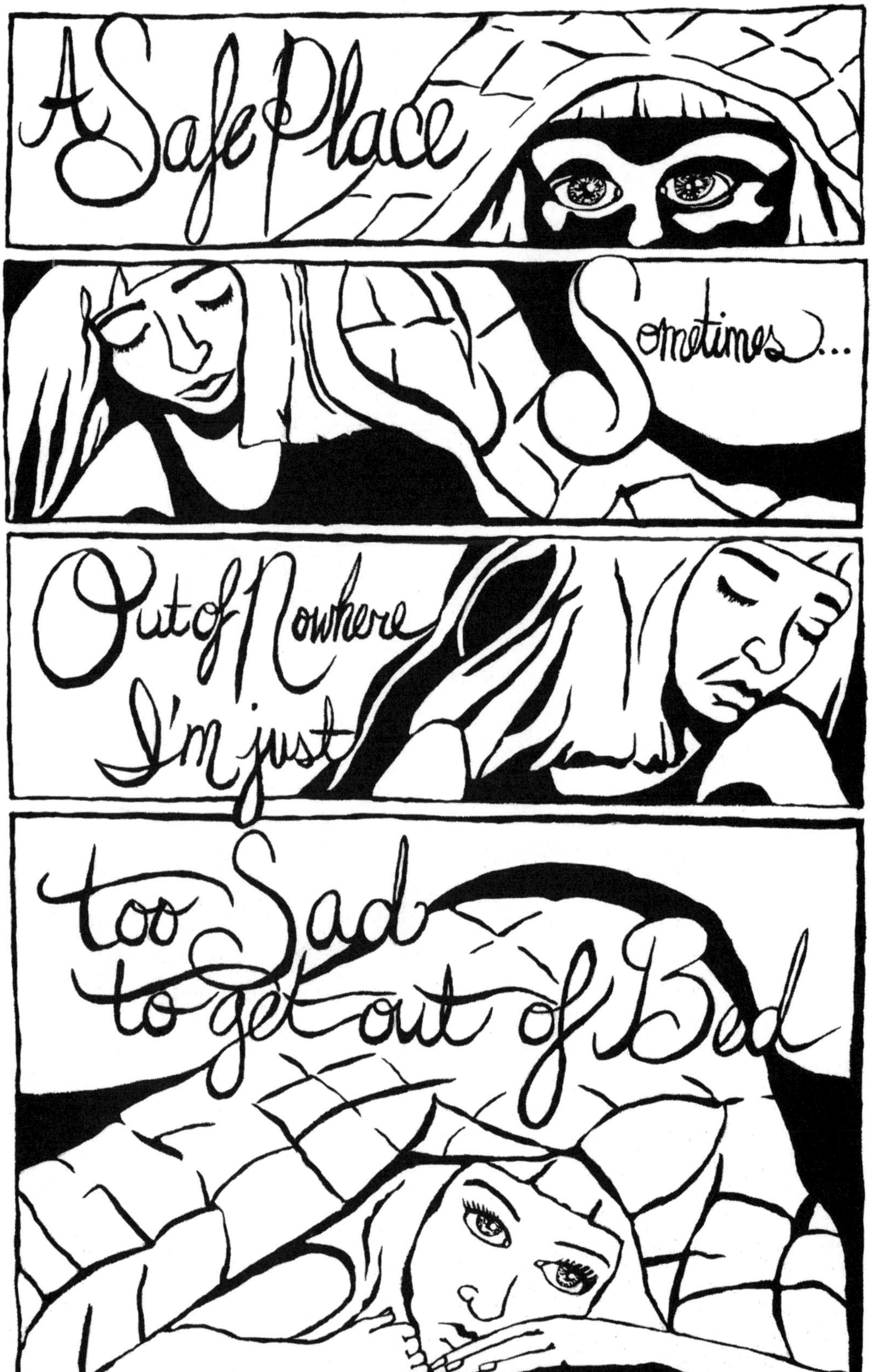
A Safe Place
Sometimes...
Out of Nowhere
I'm just
too Sad
to get out of Bed

A Safe Place

When I was little, there were monsters that used the cover of night to hide in all the dark corners of my house. If I could make it to bed, if I could cover myself entirely (hair and all) with the blankets, I would be safe.

I TELL MYSELF that it's okay to be sad.

I tell myself that I have every reason to be depressed, that the fact that I get up and do something as many days as I do is a feat.

I tell myself that I deserve a ceiling full of gold stars.

So if I need to spend a day in bed, under the covers, with an excellent book to distract me, that's okay.

And if I need to spend a day in bed, just sobbing, so the next day will be better, that's a fair trade-off.

THE DEAD BIRD

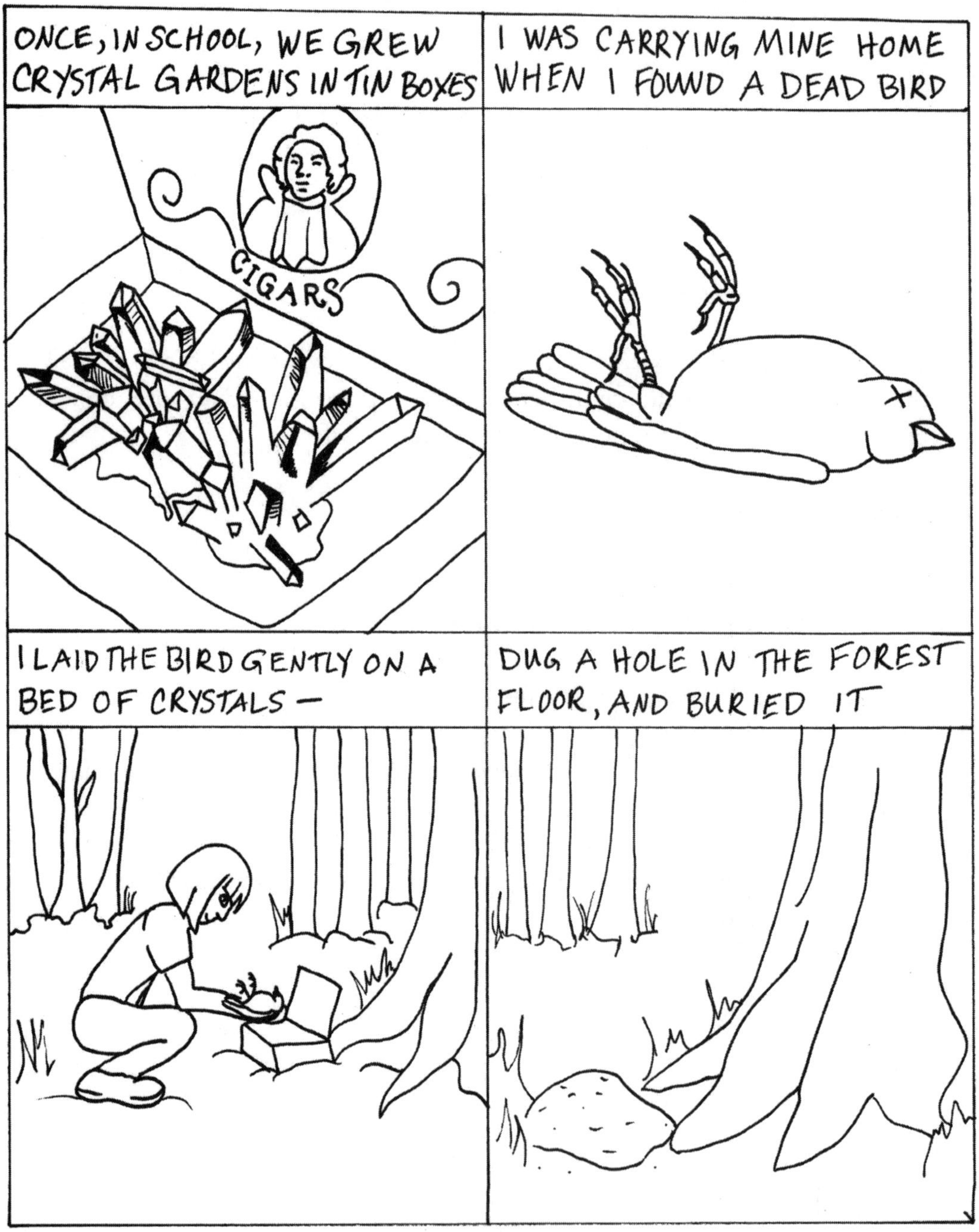
ONCE, IN SCHOOL, WE GREW CRYSTAL GARDENS IN TIN BOXES
CIGARS
I WAS CARRYING MINE HOME WHEN I FOUND A DEAD BIRD
I LAID THE BIRD GENTLY ON A BED OF CRYSTALS —
DUG A HOLE IN THE FOREST FLOOR, AND BURIED IT

The Dead Bird

Sometimes magic comes in unexpected forms.

This is a story of obvious magic, the magic of crystals grown in a left-of-centre classroom, from salts and food colouring.

This is also the story of unexpected magic. The story of a little girl finding a dead songbird on the side of the road. Of marvelling in the soft roughness of its skin, the smooth symmetry of its feathers, the dull glass of its inert eyes. This is a story of vulnerability and dignity in death.

I MUST HAVE been nine or ten years old. I was proud of the cigar box of crystals I'd grown in school, and I was carrying it home to show my mom.

I had about half a mile to walk. I'd been dropped off where my rural road met a slightly larger rural road. I took my time, walking not on the asphalt, but along the flood ditch. It had been a couple of weeks since I walked this ditch and I needed to see if anything interesting had fallen out of a car lately. One time, I'd found a metal medallion and I felt like Indiana Jones. Chokecherries grew there, and I liked to taste their bitter fruit. Farther along, blackberries crowded the ditch. For a split spring second, tiny wild strawberries appeared. But it wasn't the season to pick berries.

It was only because I was surveying my tiny kingdom so meticulously that I found the dead bird, lying on its back.

I sat down and held the bird's tiny body close. I felt its still-strong beak and the looseness of its talons in death. It weighed nothing at all. I wanted to protect it.

So I did what I could. That's what we all do, stumbling through each day as best we can, trying to live up to our own ideals of kindness and caring. To protect the bird's dignity in death, to keep it safe from marauding animals, I laid its body gently in the cigar box. I used branches to dig into the rich, peaty ground. When I could dig no more, I placed the bird in its tin coffin. I refilled the hole with earth and pine needles.

And then I walked home from school, swinging my now-empty arms, still on time.

BITE ME

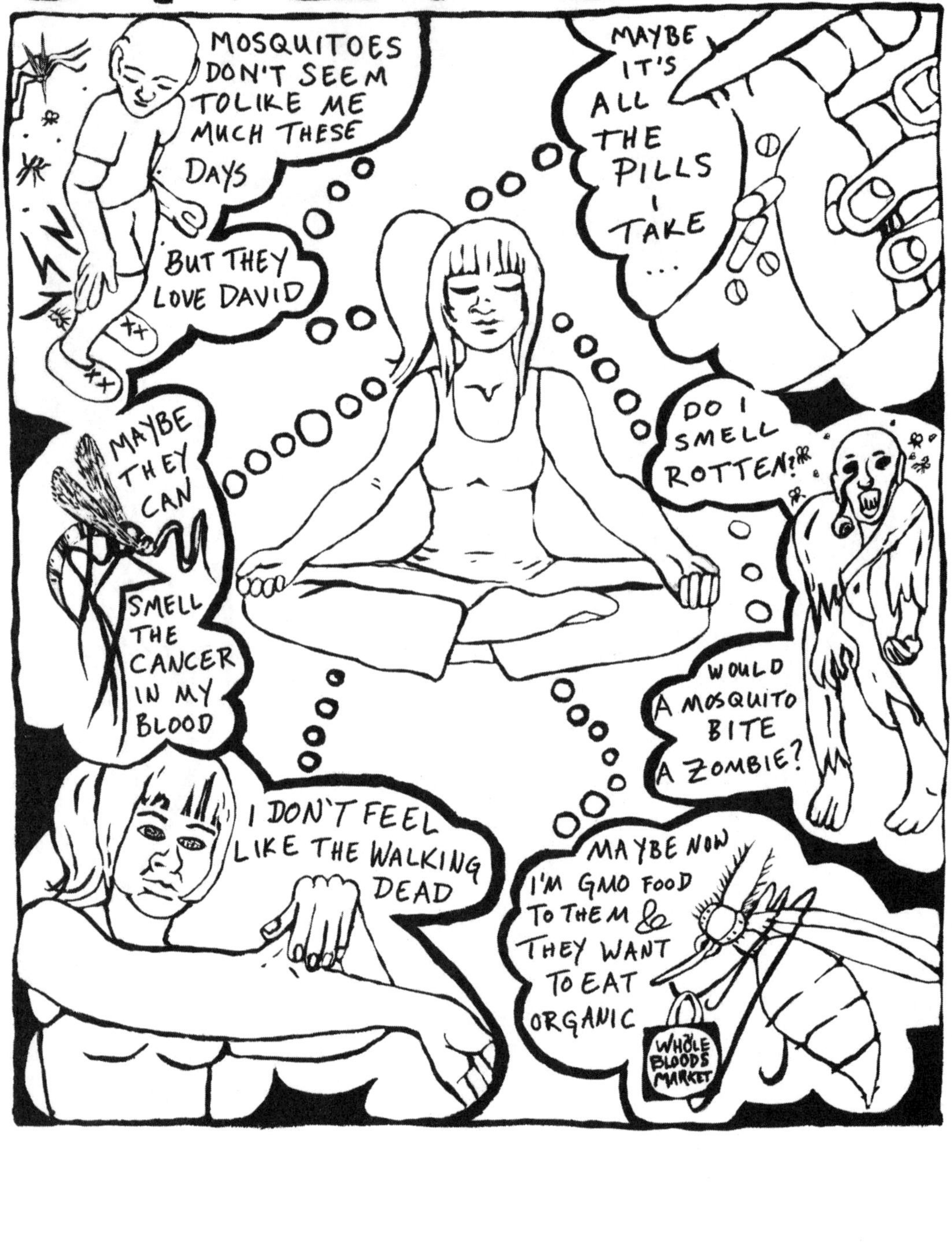
MOSQUITOES DON'T SEEM TO LIKE ME MUCH THESE DAYS
BUT THEY LOVE DAVID
MAYBE IT'S ALL THE PILLS I TAKE ...
MAYBE THEY CAN SMELL THE CANCER IN MY BLOOD
DO I SMELL ROTTEN?
WOULD A MOSQUITO BITE A ZOMBIE?
I DON'T FEEL LIKE THE WALKING DEAD
MAYBE NOW I'M GMO FOOD TO THEM & THEY WANT TO EAT ORGANIC
WHOLE BLOODS MARKET

Bite Me

Blood. The stuff of life. Flowing through my body, filtering out spent cells and delivering essential nourishment to my extremities.

Blood. Coursing through my veins, cancer cells tumbling along, looking for purchase, a place to latch on and start another metastasis.

And that same blood carries the drugs that are keeping my cancer stable. A heady cocktail of life and death, writ small.

Every month, my blood is drawn, analyzed. My participation in this current clinical trial hinges on the results.

And to the mosquito, that connoisseur of blood, how do I smell? How do I taste? Am I exotic or am I rotten? Do I make its wee stomach turn? Is there a manufactured smell about me, something less than human? Or maybe more?

What does the mosquito know about my health that I don't?

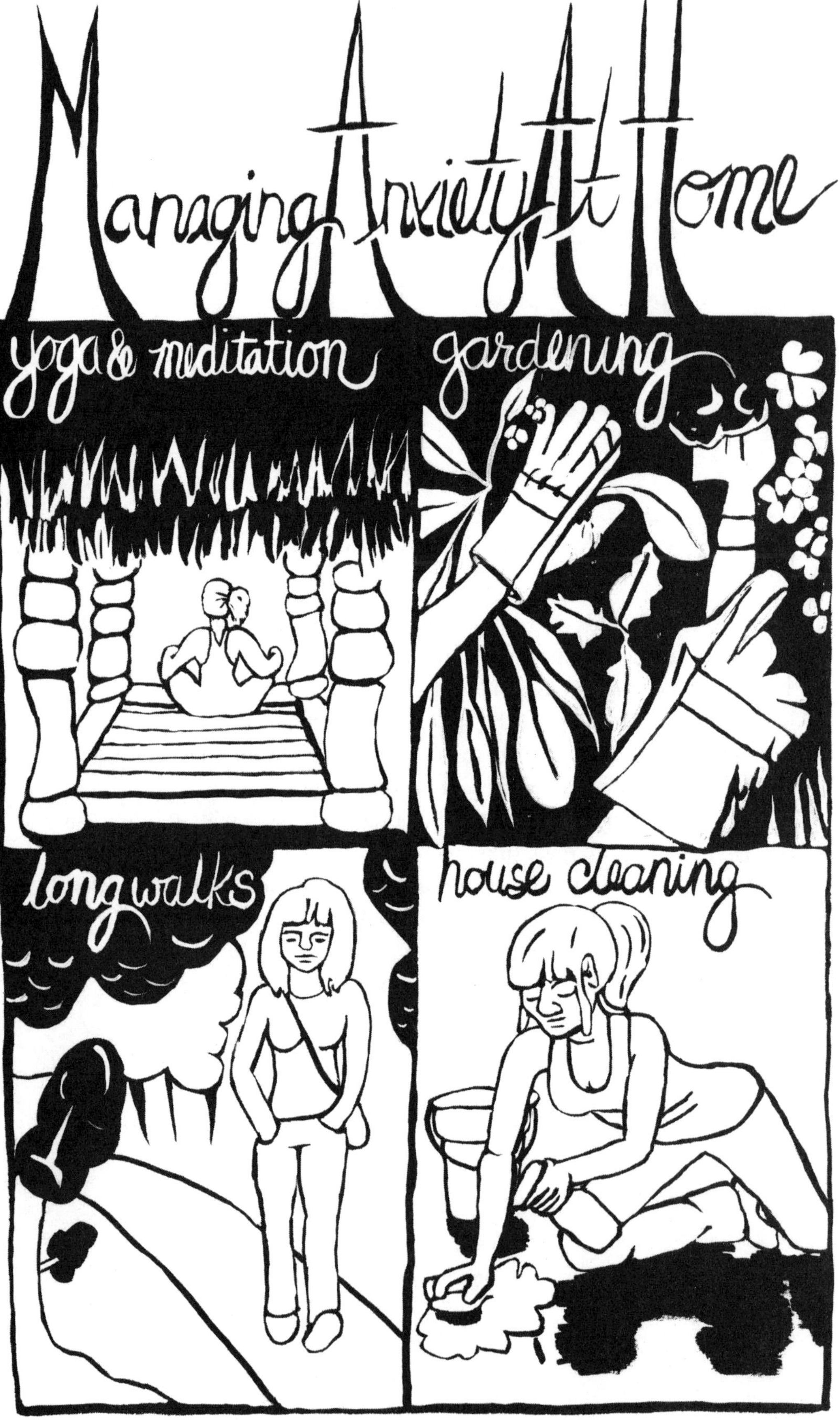
Managing Anxiety At Home
yoga & meditation
gardening
long walks
house cleaning

Managing Anxiety at Home

There's a dark, dense, tense place full of electric buzzing in my head. Anxiety lives there with depression and recrimination.

I can't let myself go there, not to stay.

I have to make myself choose the light, choose the best things I can do, the things that make me the most well in the head and centre me in my body.

It can be hard. There are days when all I can do is sleep. And there are days when I can't make myself leave the house. And I try very hard to go easy on myself about those days.

Some of the best ways I know to cut through the noise, I can do at home and I can do alone. And if I can do one of those things, I can probably do another, and it snowballs, until I feel like I can do anything.

And the days I sleep away are okay because of the other days when I do yoga, tend my thriving garden, meditate, and take a walk.

If I can do all of that, then I'm taking care of myself. I'm breathing through the anxiety or the tears, tiring my body, and eating enough.

And if I'm up late, and the noise fills my head, I can breathe through that, too.

Baby Did a Bad Thing

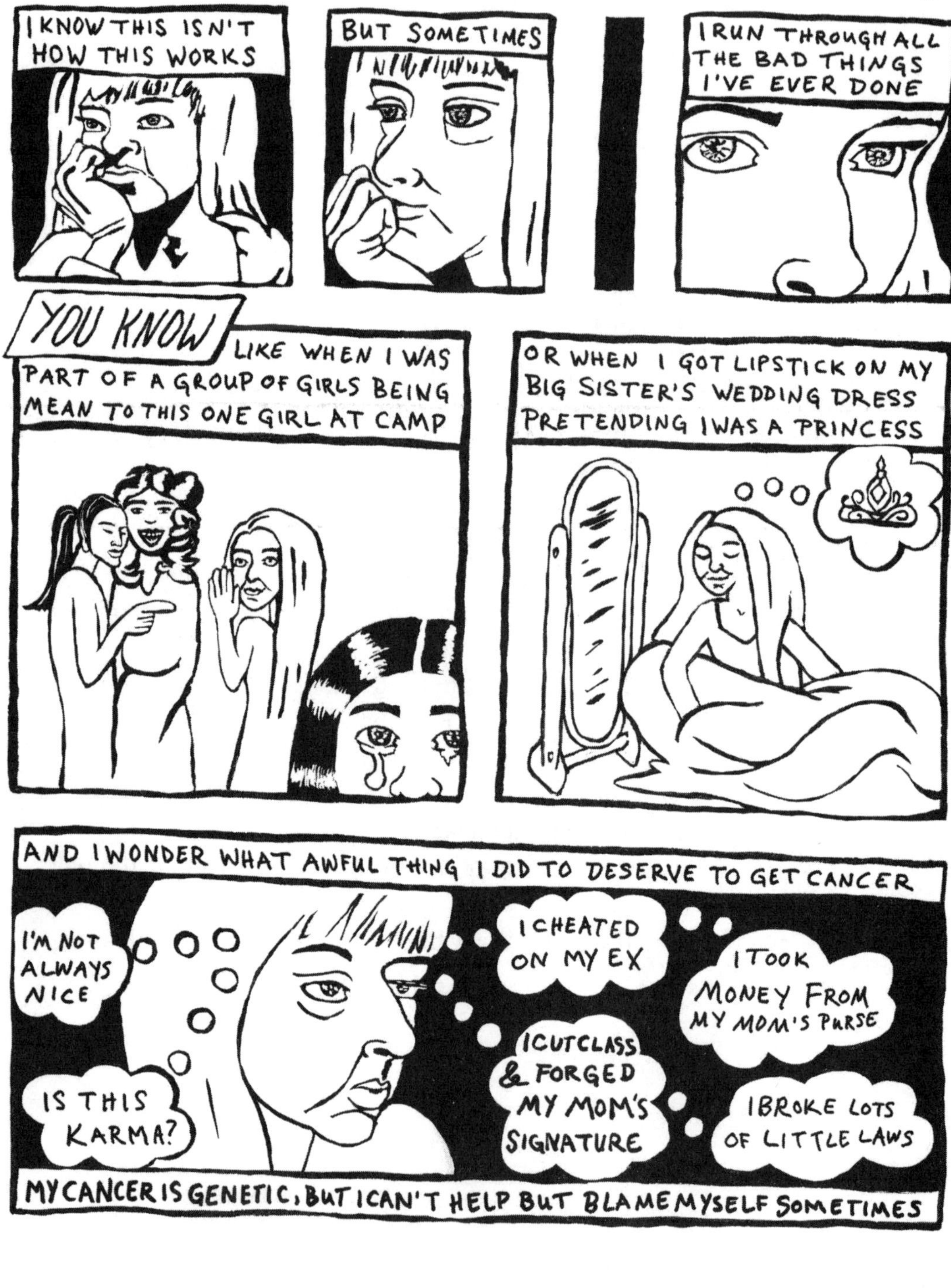

I KNOW THIS ISN'T HOW THIS WORKS
BUT SOMETIMES
I RUN THROUGH ALL THE BAD THINGS I'VE EVER DONE
YOU KNOW
LIKE WHEN I WAS PART OF A GROUP OF GIRLS BEING MEAN TO THIS ONE GIRL AT CAMP
OR WHEN I GOT LIPSTICK ON MY BIG SISTER'S WEDDING DRESS PRETENDING I WAS A PRINCESS
AND I WONDER WHAT AWFUL THING I DID TO DESERVE TO GET CANCER
I'M NOT ALWAYS NICE
I CHEATED ON MY EX
I TOOK MONEY FROM MY MOM'S PURSE
I CUT CLASS & FORGED MY MOM'S SIGNATURE
IS THIS KARMA?
I BROKE LOTS OF LITTLE LAWS
MY CANCER IS GENETIC, BUT I CAN'T HELP BUT BLAME MYSELF SOMETIMES

Baby Did a Bad Thing

There are things we know, and there are things we feel.

I know that my cancer is hereditary. Everybody agrees.

But I feel, deep in my dark places, every slight I've ever enacted upon another person. Every bad thought and every bad action. They're heavy here, in the land of cancer.

I know what I know, and I know what I feel.

I hope that the good I've tried to do, since I learned how doing bad affected others, vastly outweighs the petty cruelties of youth.

And that hope has nothing to do with my cancer and everything to do with how I want to live on, in other people.

Dreams

ALL TANGLED UP IN YOU

Happily Ever After

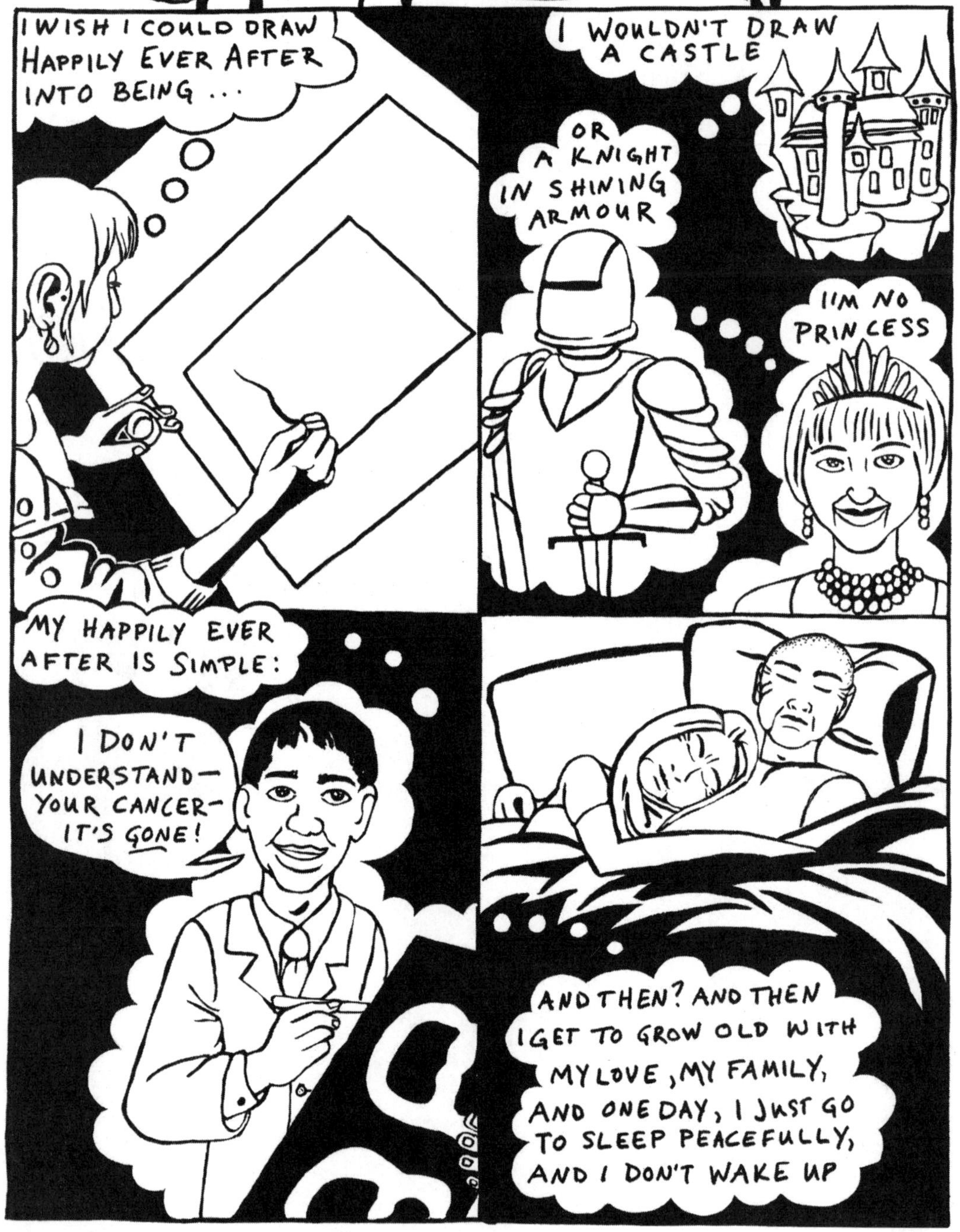
I WISH I COULD DRAW HAPPILY EVER AFTER INTO BEING...
I WOULDN'T DRAW A CASTLE
OR A KNIGHT IN SHINING ARMOUR
I'M NO PRINCESS
MY HAPPILY EVER AFTER IS SIMPLE:
I DON'T UNDERSTAND— YOUR CANCER— IT'S GONE!
AND THEN? AND THEN I GET TO GROW OLD WITH MY LOVE, MY FAMILY, AND ONE DAY, I JUST GO TO SLEEP PEACEFULLY, AND I DON'T WAKE UP

Happily Ever After

Why should I believe that I deserve more than one happily ever after? When I met David, wasn't that enough happiness for one little life? Why am I so selfish? What makes me think I'm so special?

MY DREAMS USED to extend as far as the eye could see. Sometimes I still get a glimpse of their unbounded glory out of the corner of my eye. It's a shadow of the manifest destiny I was raised to expect in my offbeat childhood at the end of the Oregon Trail.

I am so humbled by cancer. It's knocked me down a peg. Or so.

I read about clinical trials and possible advances, and I try not to let myself hope too hard. The fall is too bruising from that height. And my hopes are clumsy and ungainly.

BUT I CAN'T help it. I catch myself hoping with every fibre of my being that there will be an end to this nightmare. Even at the best moments, I'm living inside a horror show I couldn't have conceived on my own.

I mean, the very depth of this dread, I could drown in it.

I'm like a spider, shaking in fear on her pretty web every time a bird flies too close. I am always afraid.

Yet somehow, some days, I forget that I'm not supposed to let the hope out and it swells to an absolutely inappropriate size.

I am dwarfed by it.

My hopes are simple. They're all tied up in living without fear, in getting to release the coiled-up snake of fire in my stomach that burns and writhes and snaps.

And when I let my guard down and the fear or the joy comes tumbling out, these feelings are enormous after being pent up for so long. Each is an entity all its own. It's as if I've formed a golem to protect me, but it's well out of my control. I have no way of predicting what will happen next.

The Mermaid Pool

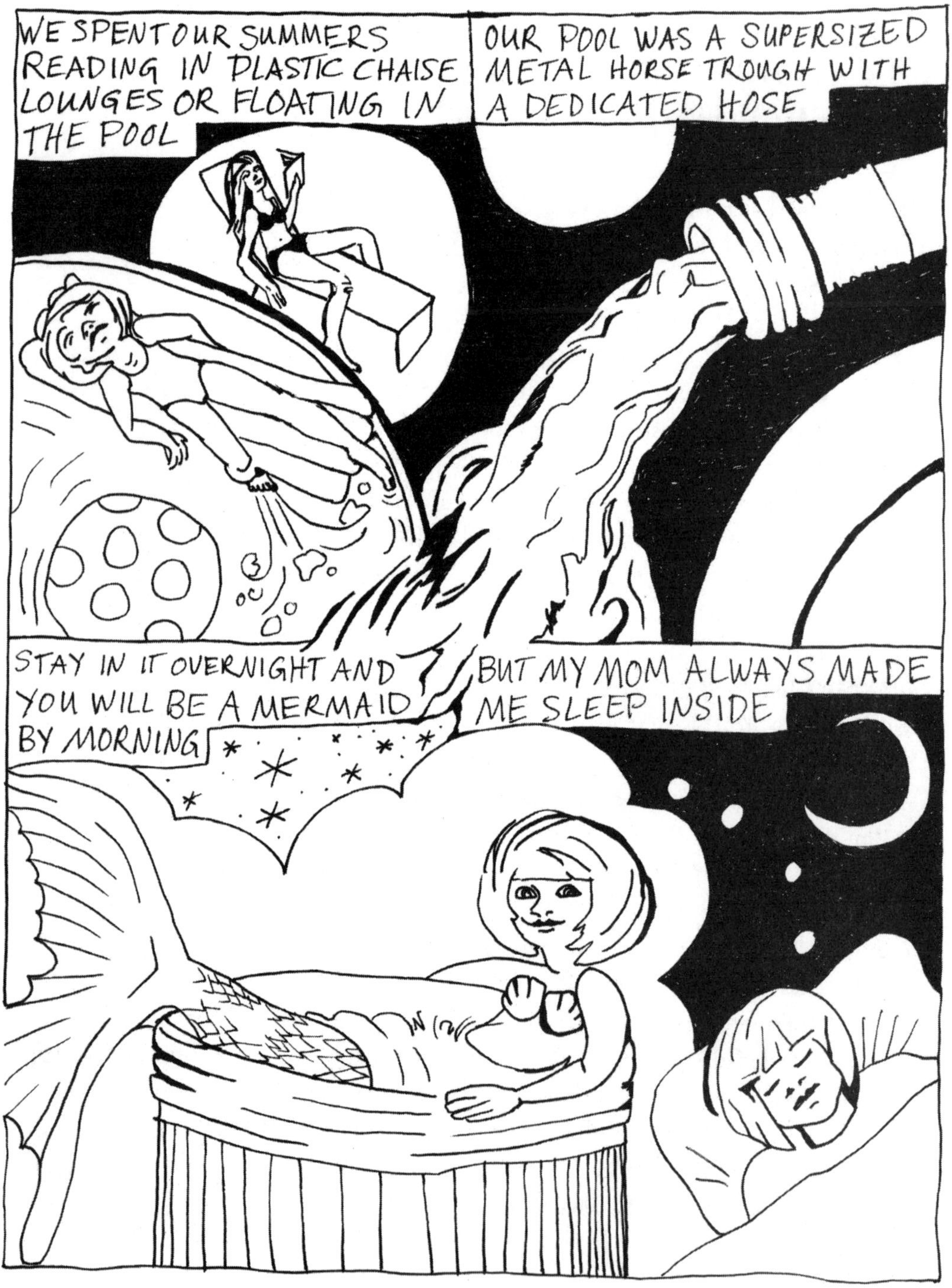
WE SPENT OUR SUMMERS READING IN PLASTIC CHAISE LOUNGES OR FLOATING IN THE POOL
OUR POOL WAS A SUPERSIZED METAL HORSE TROUGH WITH A DEDICATED HOSE
STAY IN IT OVERNIGHT AND YOU WILL BE A MERMAID BY MORNING
BUT MY MOM ALWAYS MADE ME SLEEP INSIDE

The Mermaid Pool

When I was a kid, summer stretched out forever. Two months away from school felt like an eternity. Absolutely anything could happen.

My sisters and I would spray lemon juice and hydrogen peroxide in our hair and lie in the sun, reading books for hours. We splashed in the oversized horse trough we called "the pool" and watched water bugs swim to the surface.

I stayed in the water until my hands and feet pruned over with wrinkles, until I could peel the rough bits of my heels off in pieces. I wanted to stay overnight, because I was absolutely certain that I'd be a mermaid by morning.

I never did stay the night in the pool, but I finally became a mermaid, when I went to New York to visit my old friend Cameo and we dressed up in scales and sparkles, pearls and hair extensions, and walked in the Coney Island Mermaid Parade.

The summer opens at Coney Island with the Mermaid Parade: a lurid mess of a nautically themed sideshow by the seashore. Thousands dress up in burlesque-inspired costumes and march along Surf Avenue. After an excruciatingly slow few miles, the parade finishes along the boardwalk and spills out just before Nathan's Famous Hot Dogs.

There were men wearing gigantic wigs supporting model ships, a woman dressed as a lobster, schools of fish, and more Poseidons than I could count. As in any parade, there were dance troupes and floats, classic cars and marching bands. Except that they were nothing like the all-American troupes and floats and bands of my childhood. The parade began as a family-friendly undersea wonderland and devolved into a mess of sparkly, slithery body paint and scaly breasts. Prizes were awarded, and bribing the judges was encouraged.

Cameo and I had decided to be pretty mermaids, but most of the other merfolk were the stuff of fever dreams: Day-Glo scales and shark bites, lewd smiles and suggestive props. The tiny girls who came to the parade because they loved *The Little Mermaid* adored us. We were the closest thing to Ariel in the flesh.

But context is everything. Surrounded by the wry, dark underbelly of the parade, our pretty, pretty costumes were creepy in their own way. The carnival barker who announced each marcher said of us, "It's the twins from *The Shining*, all grown up."

Being in a parade was harder than I expected. I walked all the time, but parade walking is slow. It involves posing for a ridiculous number of photographs. Your arm gets tired from waving and your cheeks hurt from smiling. Every time you pause, people hold up their cameras and shout for your attention. One camera turns into a dozen before you're free to move again. But it was something else, floating down that Coney Island street, nothing but a pretty, pretty mermaid for a few hours.

Dreams can come true, if we'll only make them.

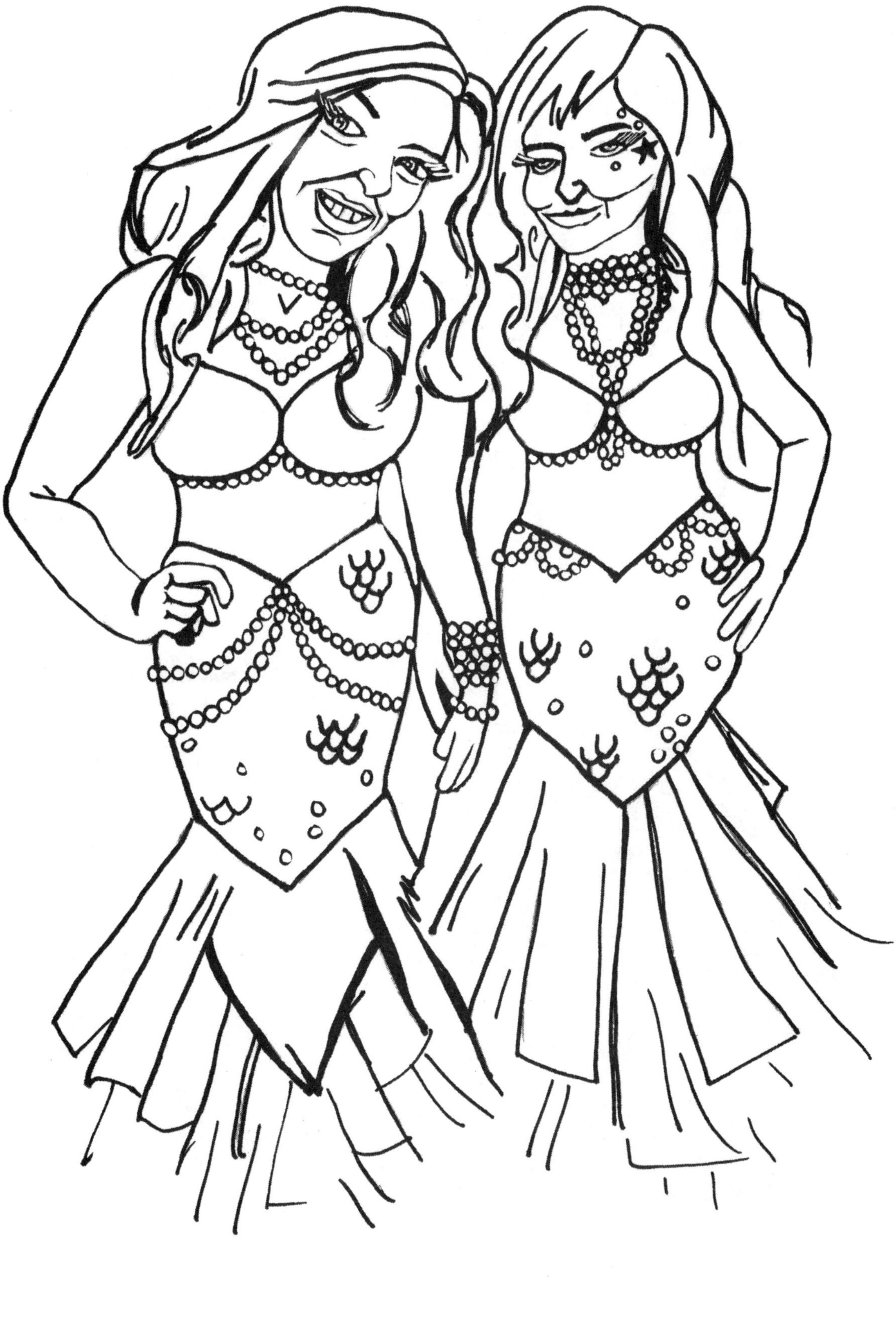
V

Incurable

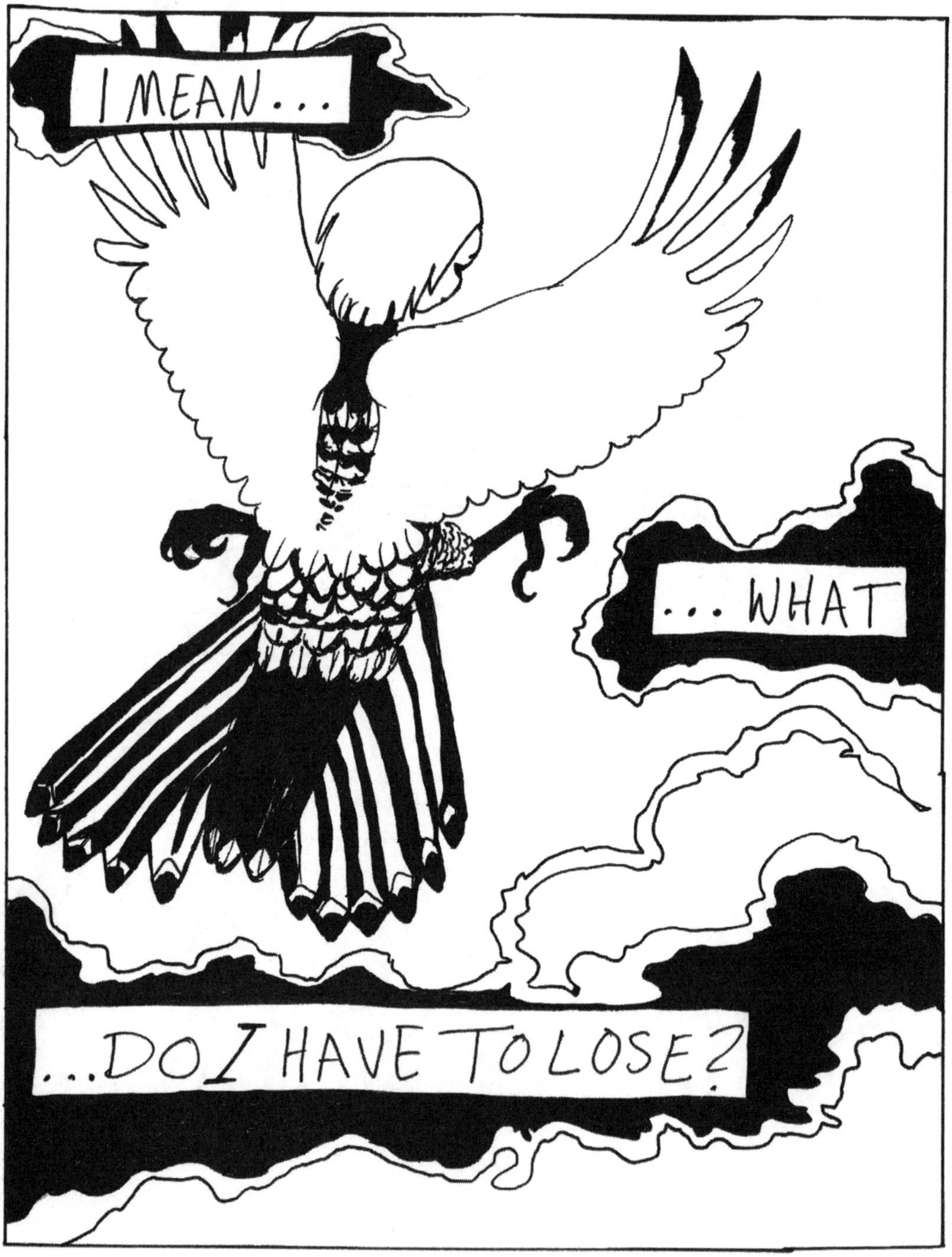
I MEAN...
...WHAT
...DO I HAVE TO LOSE?

Incurable

So. Here I am. In treatment for the rest of my life.

Really, what shouldn't I do?

What do I actually have to lose? This disease will kill me eventually, but it could be years and years and years. I have to count on that.

And in the meantime—whatever that means—I really have nothing to lose.

So I am going to say yes even more. Live like a tornado, when I can. I'm going to suck the marrow out of life and see what I've been missing.

Resources

These are a few of the organizations that have been especially helpful to me and my friends. Some are national or international organizations; some are local; all are full of dynamic, positive, generous people who are devoting their time to helping people like me. What a gift!

Metastatic Breast Cancer Network
mbcn.org

Metavivor
metavivor.org

ReThink Breast Cancer
rethinkbreastcancer.com

Young Adult Cancer Canada
youngadultcancer.ca

Canadian Breast Cancer Foundation
cbcf.org

Stretch Heal Grow
stretchhealgrow.org

Wellspring
wellspring.ca

Willow
willow.org

Acknowledgements

Never in my life have I needed so much support. The friends and family who have helped me are luminous creatures, and too legion to list. Whether it was cooking or cleaning when I wasn't up to it, helping me run errands, sitting at the hospital with me, or helping me figure out what to do with the comics that had started to pour out of my hands, I could not have made this book without a lot of help.

I am grateful to my family: Teri, Malu, Keira, Thor, Josh, Joan, Tova, Devin, and Steve, for supporting my idea to include a small memorial to their mother, sister, aunt, niece, wife, father, grandfather, and/or great-grandfather. I hope I captured something of what you loved about each of them.

Thank you to Aubrey Lindley, Jesse Manis, Cameo Morningstar, Rob Wilkinson, Meaghan Strimas, Medeine Tribinevicious, Rebecca Webster, Susan Wilk, Sean Marven, Keyla Lopez, James Beckett, Sue Harrison, Paul and Joan Harrison, Laura Warner, Juliana Vegh, James Caldwell, Ian Dyament, Scott Anderson, Shelley Ambrose, Taya Lindley, Conny and Walter Lindley, Rachel Giese, Alison Pick, Peter Birkemoe, Mark Askwith, Joshua Knelman, Samantha Haywood, Dani Couture, Stacey May Fowles, Spencer Saunders, Mary Oliver, Norma D'Agostino, Burt Eikleberry, Marilyn Frasca, Jen Saxena, Jim and Cyrilla Leonard, Tania Little, Sara Falconer, Quincin Chan, Mary Cranston, Alison Jones, Lori Kufner, Rebecca Zamon, Adam Shona, Allegra Young, George Stratigacos, Carolyn Mallory, Alexandra Molotkow, Monty Olsen, Shelagh Rogers, Veronica Thompson, Tara Hendela, Dani Mailing, Emma Jenkin, Raoul Saxena, Ryan Cuggy, Julie Wood, John Lounds, Mark Hajek, Billy Pollard, Jennifer Creagh, Melinda Cox, Mike Fuhr, Wing Yiu Chan (Sam), Ingrid Ng, Jasmin Fiore, Anna Craig, Melinda Holm, and

159

Jill Alvarez. Thanks to everybody I've met along the way in places like retreats or waiting rooms living with cancer or the effects of treatment. Thanks to my medical team, especially Dr. Phillipe Bedard, an early reader of this book, and Dr. Abdulla Al-Ozairi, who encouraged me to keep drawing. I am very lucky to have so many good people in my life and I do not take that for granted. If I haven't mentioned you here, I hope you already know how grateful I am.

I owe a huge debt of gratitude to Sarah MacLachlan, Janie Yoon, Matt Williams, Alysia Shewchuk, Laura Meyer, and everybody at Anansi for believing in this book and for being very kind and very patient with me. I feel lucky to be working with them.

Before there was a book, there were comics. Thanks to Matthew McKinnon for seeing something in them. Thanks to *The Walrus* magazine for becoming their online home. And thanks to Brian Morgan for your insight, guidance, and encouragement.

Thanks to the Ontario Arts Council for supporting this project.

And thank you to my husband David, my love, my life, and always my first reader.

ADOBE GARAMOND PRO is a digital interpretation of roman and italic types originally created in the sixteenth century. The roman type was designed in 1989 by Robert Slimbach for Adobe and is based on the designs of French printer Claude Garamond. The italics are derived from the designs of Robert Granjon, Garamond's assistant.

TRADE GOTHIC is a sans-serif typeface designed by Jackson Burke at Linotype Co. between 1948–1960. Due to the irregularities within its family structure, Trade Gothic is considered more naturalistic than other grotesques developed around that time, such as Helvetica and Univers. A typographic staple among designers, this font family is used widely in newspapers, books, and magazines.

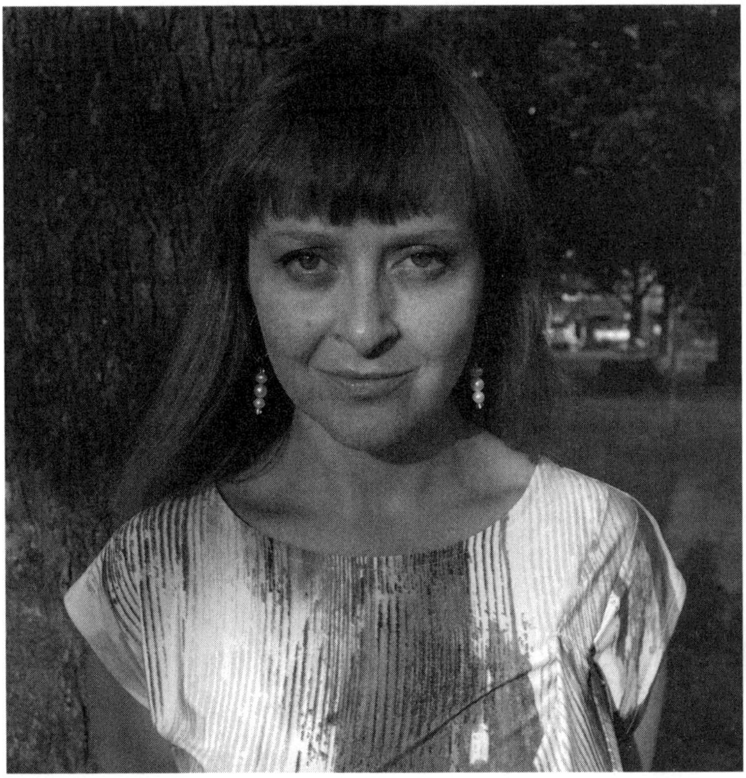

Author photograph: © David P. Leonard

TEVA HARRISON is a writer and artist. Her graphic series on living with cancer is published by *The Walrus*, and she has commented on CBC Radio and in the *Globe and Mail* about her experience. Numerous health organizations have invited her to speak publicly on behalf of the metastatic cancer community. She lives in Toronto.